SKILLS IN HISTORY

BOOK 3 · THE TWENTIETH CENTURY

NADIA

Are you doing anything special over the vacation?
I don't think
so. maybe
Italy or s. of france
but I doubt it.

Series Editor: PAUL SHUTER

PAUL SHUTER   TERRY LEWIS

 HEINEMANN EDUCATIONAL BOOKS

Heinemann Educational Books Ltd
Halley Court, Jordan Hill, Oxford OX2 8EJ

OXFORD   LONDON   EDINBURGH
MELBOURNE   SYDNEY   AUCKLAND
SINGAPORE   MADRID   IBADAN   NAIROBI
GABORONE   HARARE   KINGSTON
PORTSMOUTH (NH)USA

First published 1988
Reprinted 1988 (with amendments), 1989

British Library Cataloguing in Publication Data

Shuter, Paul
    Skills in history.
    Bk. 3: The twentieth century
    1.History
    I. Title II. Lewis, Terry
    900   D21
ISBN 0-435-31864-0

Designed and typeset by
The Pen and Ink Book Company Ltd, London

Printed in Great Britain by
Butler & Tanner, Frome and London

ISBN 0 435 31867 5
(Teacher's Set)

Other titles in the *Skills in History* series:

Book 1 Changes
An introductory section explains what chronology is,
how historians work, the clues they look for, the
differences between primary and secondary sources and how
they are used. There are further sections on the Romans,
Saxons, Normans and Tudors.

Book 2 Revolutions
This book looks at two different types of revolution; one
political, the other economic. Part One covers England in
the seventeenth century. Part Two describes Britain's
Industrial Revolution.

Contents

PART THREE SOME MODERN WORLD PROBLEMS

PART FOUR SOURCES

Acknowledgements

The authors and publishers would like to thank the following for permission to reproduce photographs on the pages indicated:

Associated Newspapers plc and the Centre for the study of Cartoons and Caricature: pp. 37 (*top*), 41, 44, 49, 51 (*top/middle*), 52, 58 and 64.
Associated Press: pp. 88, 102 (*top*) and 104 (*top*).
Colin Atkins: p. 7.
BBC Hulton Picture Library: pp. 10 (*top*), 11, 12 (*top*), 15, 22 (*top*), 26, 33 (*top*), 35, 48 and 106.
Belfast Telegraph: p. 115.
Bildarchiv Süddeutscher Verlag: pp. 34 and 75.
British Library: p. 96.
British Library, Newspaper Library: p. 13.
Camera Press: pp. 62 (*top/upper middle/lower*), 85, 91, 108 (*top*), 110, 114 and 120 (*lower*).
Carl Frank, Photo Researchers, New York: p. 76.
Essex Record Office: p. 22 (*lower*).
Franklin D. Roosevelt Library: p. 31 (*left*).
Henry Ford Museum and Greenfield Village: p. 29 (*lower*).
IDAF: pp. 108 (*lower*) and 109.
Imperial Tobacco plc: p. 51 (*lower left*).
Imperial War Museum: pp. 4 (*left*), 6, 8, 10 (*lower*), 12 (*middle/lower*), 51 (*lower right*) and 59.
John Hillelson Agency: p. 93 (*lower*).
The Kobal Collection: p. 29 (*top*).
Library of Congress: p. 22 (*middle*).
Mansell Collection: p. 4 (*right*).
Mary Evans Picture Library: p. 16 (*lower*).
Moro, Roma: p. 33 (*middle*).
NAAS: p. 104 (*lower*).
NASA: pp. 63 (*top*) and 83.
Novosti Press Agency: p. 17 (*right*).
Oxfam: p. 63 (*lower*).
Palach Press: p. 93 (*top*).
Judah Passow/Network: p. 80.
Popperfoto: pp. 61, 69, 74, 82, 95 (*left*) and 120 (*top*).
Public Record Office: p. 56.
Punch Publications: pp. 9 and 112.
Rizzoli Photographic Archive: p. 33 (*lower*).
Society for Cultural Relations with the USSR: p. 24.
John Sturrock/Network: p. 117.
Gordon Thomas and Max Morgan-Witts/Jonathan Clowes: p. 47.
Topham: pp. 31(*right*), 62 (*lower middle*), 77, 95 (*right*) and 102 (*lower*).
United States Air Force: p. 79.
Roger Viollet: p. 38.
Wiener Library: p. 37 (*lower*).

1
Events 1900–20

In 1900 the countries of Europe, together with the United States and Japan, dominated the **world**. They were stronger than any other states, and they **ruled** much of the rest of the world through their colonies. **Source A** shows the extent of their influence, and Source B shows the relative size of the powers and their empires.

The great powers were suspicious of each other, and made alliances with one another for safety. Germany was a fairly new country; it had only existed since 1870, and its neighbours were worried that if it continued to grow it would become the greatest power in the world. The powers settled into two groups. The **Triple Alliance** linked Germany, the Austrian Empire, and Italy; the **Triple Entente** (*entente* is French for understanding) brought together Britain, France and Russia. The terms of these agreements were secret. One side could not know exactly what countries on the other side would do to support each other.

In western Europe, France had lost land (Alsace Lorraine) to Germany after a war in 1870; most Frenchmen wanted it back. In eastern Europe the Turkish empire was falling apart. The people who lived in the Balkans (those countries of eastern Europe which had been ruled by the Turks) wanted to be independent. Russia and Austria, however, both wanted to gain power in the area (and to stop the other doing so). Britain and Germany added to the tension by having a 'naval race'. They both spent vast sums building the new superweapon, battleships called *Dreadnoughts*. This naval race was linked to quarrels that the powers had about their colonies. Germany started late in the race to gain colonies, but was trying hard to catch up.

The 'trigger' which set off the events leading up to the First World War happened in the Balkans. The Archduke Franz Ferdinand, next in line to the Austrian throne, was assassinated in Sarajevo. The assassins had some contact with **Serbia**, a newly independent state in the Balkans. Austria (backed and encouraged by Germany) used the assassination as an excuse to humiliate Serbia; Serbia (encouraged by Russia) resisted. Austria declared war on Serbia (28 July). Russia **mobilised** its army (got it ready to fight) which caused the Germans to declare war on Russia (1 August). As Russia was allied to France the Germans also declared war on France (3 August). The Germans had long been afraid that they would not be able to win a war in which they fought France and Russia, and they had become convinced that if

Source A

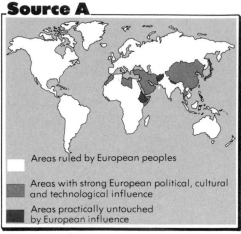

Areas ruled by European peoples

Areas with strong European political, cultural and technological influence

Areas practically untouched by European influence

Europe's influence over the rest of the world in 1900.

Source B

		Size of country (miles^2)	Size of overseas empire (miles^2)
1	Great Britain	120,979	10,500,000
2	Russia	8,660,395	
3	France	204,092	4,367,000
4	USA	2,939,000	620,000
5	Germany	208,830	1,000,000
6	Austria-Hungary	264,204	
7	Italy	110,646	185,000
8	Japan	147,655	14,000

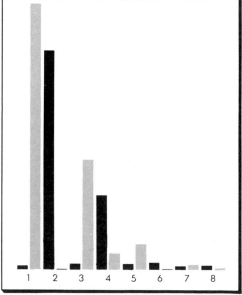

The size of the major powers and their empires.

this happened they must quickly defeat France and then turn on Russia. This was called the **Schlieffen Plan**. The Germans believed it was their only hope of winning the war. France had strong defences on its borders with Germany, so the plan was to attack France through Belgium. Britain had a treaty with Belgium, and when the Germans invaded Belgium, Britain entered the war on the side of France and Russia (4 August).

The Schlieffen Plan nearly worked. The Germans got to within 40 miles of Paris, but then were turned back. The war in France (**the Western Front**) then ceased to move. Both sides dug trench systems and neither could break through. In the East, however, the Germans won important victories over the Russians. The Russians lost so much vital military equipment in these defeats that, although they still had over six million men in their army, one-third of them did not have rifles.

During 1915 neither side could find a way of breaking the deadlock on the Western Front. Britain and its allies tried to invade Gallipoli in eastern Europe; this would have kept their communications with Russia safe, and perhaps given a base for a new attack on Germany. The plan failed with about 200,000 casualties. Turkey had joined the war on Germany's side at the end of 1914, but this was evened out when Italy joined the Allies in May 1915.

In 1916 there were two major battles on the Western Front, **Verdun** and the **Somme**. The losses in the two battles were staggering (France 509,000; Germany 930,000; Britain 418,000), and neither battle led to a breakthrough. At sea there was also a major battle, off Jutland. This was the first time the main German fleet had left port and,

after Jutland, it returned home and did not leave port again during the war.

Since 1915 the Germans had been trying to starve Britain out of the war by using submarines to sink vital supply ships. In 1917 the Germans announced their submarines would attack any ships, even those from a neutral country. This tipped the balance in the United States, which entered the war on the side of the Allies on 6 April 1917. In the same year though, there were two revolutions in Russia. After the second, the Russians pulled out of the war.

1918 began with a race. Would the Germans get their troops from the East to the Western Front quickly enough to win the war, or would the Americans arrive in time? The Germans made a major attack which finally broke through the trenches, but again they were stopped short of Paris, and this time American troops were flooding into France to keep pushing the Germans back. The German generals realised that they could not win the war, and that an invasion of Germany was only a matter of time, so they advised their government to take up the American President's offer to act as a peacemaker. On 11 November 1918 the war was finally over.

The Germans believed the war had been ended on a plan suggested by Woodrow Wilson (the American President) called the Fourteen Points. Britain and France, however, had other ideas about what they wanted from a peace. In fact the peace treaties of 1919 were not negotiated with the defeated countries, but imposed on them by the victors. Many of the terms of the treaties seemed unfair to the losers, especially to the Germans, and they were to cause much trouble in Europe in the next twenty years.

Questions

Section A

1 Which country had the largest empire in 1900?

2 Which major powers had no empires in 1900?

3 List the great powers in order of size, with the biggest first, counting only the size of the countries not the empires.

4 Make another list of the powers in order of size, but this time count the empires and the countries themselves.

5 Why do you think empires were important to the powers?

6 The First World War is called a **world** war, yet there was hardly any fighting outside Europe. Why do you think it was called a world war?

Section B

7 Draw a time-line showing the various events mentioned in the text.

8 Historians often divide history up into sections or periods because it makes it easy to think about. Mark three different periods on your time-line and say why you have chosen to make the divisions where you have.

First Reactions to the War

On 1 and 2 August, Germany declared war on France and Russia. The German plan was for a quick victory over France in the west, completed in time for its armies to turn east to fight the Russians. The need for speed meant the Germans intended to attack France through Belgium, and this invasion of neutral Belgium was the reason given for Britain's declaration of war at 11pm on 4 August.

We live in an age when the idea of a major war has been a horror too great almost to think about, and news that war has been declared would not be received with much happiness now. This was not the case in 1914. The declarations of war were received with great shows of public support in most European countries. There were mass demonstrations, celebrations as troops left for the war, and recruits came flooding in.

In Britain Lord Kitchener, the minister for war, called for 100,000 new recruits to serve in the army for the duration of the war. He called for a second 100,000 before the end of the month, and by mid September 500,000 men had joined up. While this was happening 125,000 soldiers, most of Britain's full-time professional army, were sent to France to join in the fighting. This army arrived as the Germans were driving the French back towards Paris, and the first two battles it fought were part of the retreat. In comparison with the German and French armies this was a very small force (the Germans had about 1,125,000 men), and the Kaiser called it a 'contemptible little army'.

Back in Britain the new recruits, who already outnumbered the pre-war army, needed to be clothed, trained and armed. This was a major problem for the army to cope with, and it would be many months before the recruits would be ready to help in France.

Source A

Source B

'That afternoon I decided to join the Liverpool Scottish. What sights I saw on my way up to Frazer Street; a queue of men over two miles long, the recruiting office took over a week to pass in all those thousands. At the Liverpool Scottish HQ it seemed hopeless; in fact I was giving up hopes of ever getting in, when I saw Rennison [an officer] and he invited me into the mess, getting me in front of hundreds of others.'

Lionel Ferguson describes the afternoon of 5 August in Liverpool.

Source C

G. R.

Your King and Country need You

A CALL TO ARMS

An addition of 100,000 men to His Majesty's Regular Army is immediately necessary in the present grave National Emergency.

Lord Kitchener is confident that this appeal will be at once responded to by all those who have the safety of our Empire at heart.

TERMS OF SERVICE.

General Service for the period of the war only. Any men so enlisting will be discharged with all convenient speed as soon as the war is over.

Age of enlistment between 19 and 30.

HOW TO JOIN.

Full information can be obtained at any Post Office or Labour Exchange in the Kingdom or at any Military Barrack.

GOD SAVE THE KING.

Newspaper advert, early August 1914.

Recruits waiting in a London churchyard, 1914.

Source D

'We had been brought up to believe that Britain was the best country in the world and we wanted to defend her. The history taught us at school showed that we were better than other people (didn't we always win the last war) now all the news was that Germany was the aggressors and we wanted to show the Germans what we could do.'

Private George Morgan's memories of why he joined up.

Source E

'Rumours of war broke out. Although I seldom saw a newspaper, I knew about the assassination of Archduke Ferdinand at Sarajevo. Towards the end of August 1914 I presented myself to the recruiting sergeant. The sergeant asked me my age and when told, replied, "Clear off, son. Come back tomorrow and see if you are nineteen, eh?" So I turned up again next day and gave my age as nineteen. Holding up my right hand I swore to fight for King and Country. The sergeant winked as he gave me the King's shilling. I was sixteen years and seven months old.'

From George Coppard, 'With a Machine Gun to Cambrai'.

Source F

In January 1915 12,000 recruits paraded in front of Kitchener and the French minister of war.

'All Friday morning it snowed, and in the afternoon it rained. We left at 11 a.m. Of course the roads were awful, thick slush and mud, and naturally everyone had their boots full of water. Long before we had marched the seven miles to the parade ground most of us were wet to the skin.

Well, we got to the ground at 1.30 p.m. Kitchener did not turn up until 4 p.m. and then only went by in a closed car and we did not see him.

Those 2 hours standing in water and slush over our ankles, wet through, with a biting wind driving sleet and heavy rain was about the nearest attempt to hell I have so far experienced.

The only recreation was to count the people who fainted and were carried out. The engineers won with 32.

12,000 men had been brought out 7 miles from home with one ambulance wagon to hold 6. The others had to lie in the slush, almost covered, until help arrived. Of course some suffered from exposure, fortunately only two died.'

Second Lieutenant Ian Melhuish, Somerset Light Infantry, writing home to his mother.

Questions

Section A

1 Why do you think Kitchener was advertising for men to join the army?

2 Does Source A **prove** that men from all classes joined the army?

3 What is there in Source C to encourage men to join the army?

4 How successful do you think Kitchener's campaign to get recruits for the army was?

5 If you had to pick one piece of evidence which best shows people's attitude to the outbreak of war, what would it be? Give reasons for your answer.

6 The writer of Source D suggests there was some connection between the history he had learned at school and his decision to join the army.

   a Do you think this can be true?

   b Do you think this type of history teaching is a good idea? Give reasons for your answer.

Section B

7 Lying and cheating are not usually thought of as good things, yet Lionel Ferguson (Source B) and George Coppard (Source E) don't mind admitting to them. Why do you think this is?

8 How do you think the recruits in Sources A, B, D and E would have felt if the war had finished before Christmas (as many people thought at the time would happen)? Give reasons for your answer.

9 How do you think Lieutenant Melhuish (Source F) felt about the war and the army after the events he describes? Give reasons for your answer.

Tommy Atkins's War

The experiences of soldiers (often called 'Tommies') in the trenches during the First World War were not what the men who had joined up in 1914 had expected. Those who survived carried the memory of this horror with them for the rest of their lives. This section uses the diary kept by one soldier, Private Sidney Atkins, to see what serving on the Western Front really meant. The diary covers the months December 1915 to August 1916 in detail. It is too long to print completely, but the selections here have been made in months to avoid just picking out days when something unusual happened.

'December 1915

… went to Gouneham for eight days rest then came to Vermailles Position.

Diary of War

9 Dec   Vermailles Position. Shell busted on parapet and blew my pack to pieces.

12 Dec   Stafford's relieved us, went to Anneque for two days.

14 Dec   Relieved 1st Kings at Maison Rouge dug-outs. Guard night and day.

16 Dec   Royal Berks. relieved us, we went to Bethume at Barrack (on fatigue next day). Unloading motor vans & loading.

18 Dec   Had a bathing parade.

19 Dec   Route March and Church Parade.

21 Dec   Firing on range at Bethume 10 Pts. in 5 rounds.

16 Dec   Going to make an attack by gas & bombers to take the front line, but it was cancelled.

21 Dec   Route March through Annezin a small village on the outskirts of Bethune. A Bombardment still taking place by our artillery to try and break the brick stacks on the brickfields, one of the hottest parts of the line. The bombardment lasted four hours and done damage.

22 Dec   went to Latouruaire for 5 mile route march. Made an attack at Latasse or Brickfields.

23 Dec   digging trenches when on rest (all day).

24 Dec   went on long route march 12 miles. Hesdinguel (aerodrome). Small village outskirts of Bethume (behind firing line nearly all are coal miners for observations posts.)

25 Dec   Christmas Day went for a route march about 5 kilometres.

26 Dec   Boxing Day. Church Parade then after drill etc. (including saluting).

27 Dec   left Bethune for divisional rest 11 miles 4 hours walk arrived at Ham a small village just 2 kilometres from Lillen our billets was in an old barn next to pigs.

28 Dec   saluting parade & Drill etc for 1 ½ hours.

29 Dec   Parades on Drill [Fire]

30 31 Dec   Drill etc. & route march.

June 1916

June 27   got relieved from guard also Factory Keep and went to Rags Keep No. 7 Platoon relieved us when we got to Rags Keep went on guard at Factory Keep we got heavy shelling.

June 28   guard (British Offensive started.) got relieved at 4 o/c & went to Vielle Chappelle.

June 29   Stand to nearly all day, shifting from one place to another.

June 30   in the morning Royal Sussex made an attack then we had to go in Reserve Billets, at night, 9-30 went to trenches in Reserve at Richburg St Basst perhaps Germans to counter attack at night we was building trenches & parapets that were blown in we got relieved on June 1st and went back to our Reserve Billets …

August 1916

August 1st   moved from Bethune to trenches from 5 o/c to 11 o/c relieved Royal Sussex on No 22 islands

August 2nd   periscope duty & guard at night

August 3rd   guard

August 4th   Periscope duty & guard at 11 o/c got relieved by No. 1 Company and went back to O.B.L guard at 12 o/c.

August 5th   guard at day & night

August 6th   Guard at day & fatigue at night from 9 o/c till 12 o/c in Shetland Rd.

August 7th   Guard at day then at 5 o/c in full marching order went on guard at 72B post. Relieved the Cambridgeshires.'

Source B

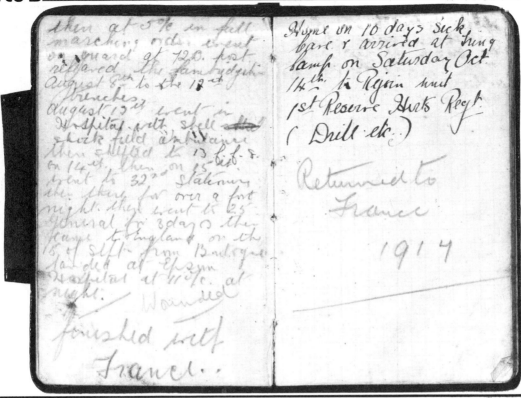

Questions

Section A

1 Make a list of all the different things Sidney Atkins did during these months of service on the Western Front.

2 How many days out of these three months did Sidney Atkins spend in the Front Line?

3 Draw a graph or pie chart to show how Sidney Atkins spent his time during the three months the diary covers here.

4 Describe the scene in Source A as closely as you can. What is each of the men doing? What are all the objects which can be seen in the picture and what could they be used for?

Section B

5 Do you think Source A shows one of the trenches Sidney Atkins served in? Give reasons for your answer.

6 At no time in the diary does Sidney Atkins tell us how he feels. There is no entry which says I felt happy today, or I felt sad today, etc. Does this mean the diary never gives any clues as to how Atkins felt?

7 Source B is a photograph of the last two pages of the diary. It starts with the entry for 7 August.
   Using the Entry for 7 August as a clue transcribe (write out) the rest of the page.

8 Do you think all of these entries were written at the same time? Give reasons for your answer.

9 Is it any easier to work out what Sidney Atkins was feeling when you look at the diary in his own handwriting?

10 When faced with a source like Sidney Atkins's diary historians have the following problems:
   • to read what the author wrote;
   • to understand what the author meant;
   • to know whether the source is reliable or not;
   • to discover whether it is useful for them or not.

   a Explain each of these problems, using the diary as an example.

   b Which of these problems do you think is the most important for the historian to solve? Give reasons for your answer.

Propaganda

I t is a fairly normal human reaction to try to get other people on your side. Just as schoolboys fighting in the playground may tell stories about one another to gain support, so countries at war often spread stories about their opponents. The correct word to describe doing this is **propaganda**. It is the deliberate spreading of stories or ideas which are intended to influence what people think.

During the First World War all the countries involved used propaganda. It could be used to get men to join the army, encourage the troops, and encourage people at home. The enemy could be made to seem utterly evil, and problems in the war could be minimised while successes were concentrated on. At the same time, propaganda could be aimed at other countries, justifying the war and trying to get those countries to join in.

The following extracts show the sort of thing that happened early in the war:

Source B

CANNON-FODDER—AND AFTER.

KAISER (to 1917 *Recruit*). "AND DON'T FORGET THAT YOUR KAISER WILL FIND A U[SE] FOR YOU—ALIVE OR DEAD."

Source A

From 'Kölnische Zeitung', a German newspaper.

'When the fall of Antwerp became known, the church bells were rung [in Cologne (Köln) and other parts of Germany].'

From 'Le Matin', a French newspaper.

'According to the *Kölnische Zeitung* the clergy at Antwerp were compelled to ring the church bells when the fortress was taken.'

From 'Corriere della Sera', an Italian newspaper.

'According to what *The Times* has heard from Cologne, via Paris, the unfortunate Belgian priests who refused to ring the church bells when Antwerp was taken, have been sentenced to hard labour.'

From 'Le Matin'.

'According to information which has reached the *Corriere della Sera* from Cologne, via London, it is confirmed that the barbaric conquerors of Antwerp punished the unfortunate Belgian priests for their heroic refusal to ring the church bells by hanging them as living clappers to the bells with their heads down.'

Extracts collected by Robert Graves in 'Goodbye To All That'.

Activities

1 In whose favour might you expect a German, Italian and French newspaper to be biased?

2 How does the story change between the first newspaper and the second?

3 How does the story change in the third newspaper?

4 How does the story change in the fourth newspaper?

5 Which, if any, of these newspaper stories do you think is reliable?

6 Do you think any of these newspaper stories will be useful to historians?

7 Is the final story from *Le Matin* biased? If so, how can you tell?

8 What effect do you think each story would have on its reader, and what effect do you think it was supposed to have had?

Source C

ARE YOU IN LEAGUE WITH THE KAISER?

FOOD WASTERS, LUXURY USERS, AND BUYERS OF USELESS ARTICLES.

(EXTRAVAGANT ONES)
"YES! War or no War, We live as Usual."

(THE KAISER)
"Thank you, my Friends, for you are indeed my Friends."

NATIONAL SERVICE

Source E

'Out of their own mouths, the military masters of Germany stand convicted of an act of unspeakable savagery which has shocked the whole civilized world. Attila's Huns were guilty of atrocious crimes, but they never desecrated the bodies of dead soldiers – their own flesh as well as the enemy – by making a factory for the conversion of human corpses into fat and oils, and fodder for pigs.'

From a Department of Information pamphlet, 1917.

Source D

'The story swept the world and, being gullible, we in the trenches were taken in by it for a while. It said that the Germans were short of fats to make glycerine. To overcome this shortage a secret factory had been set up in the Black Forest, to which the bodies of dead British soldiers were despatched. The bodies, wired together in bundles, were pitchforked onto conveyor belts and moved into the factory for conversion into fats. War artists and cartoonists got busy, and dreadful scenes were drawn and published in Britain. The effect on me was one of morbid despondency. Death was not enough apparently. The idea of finishing up in a stew pot was bloody awful, but as I had so many other problems the story soon lost its effect on me.'

From George Coppard, 'With a Machine Gun to Cambrai'.

Propaganda is clearly difficult for historians to use. As it was often designed to mislead people at the time, it is sometimes very hard to work out the truth from it. However, the propaganda of the First World War is an important source for historians of the war. It was part of the war for the people who lived through it, and we can only know what people thought and felt about the war when we know what they were told about it. If a Frenchman, who read the story about the priests being killed by being used as clappers in bells, was made so angry by the story that he went and joined the army, then the story is important, **even if it did not happen**.

Questions

Section A

1 What things was propaganda expected to do during the First World War?

2 For each of Sources B–E, say whether it is an example of propaganda and, if it is propaganda, what its aim was.

Section B

3 There was no factory converting bodies into fats in Germany. Does this mean a historian will not find Source D useful?

4 Give an example of something a historian could use Source B for, where Source B would be a reliable source.

5 Give an example of something a historian could try to use Source B for, where Source B would not be a reliable source.

6 Is it true that for a historian the only sources that are useful are those which are true? Explain your answer using examples from this unit.

The Home Front

The First World War was not over quickly, as all the experts had expected. It became a long drawn out struggle as the Great Powers tried to win by exhausting the enemy. If Britain was to continue to be able to fight then events on the 'Home Front' were just as important as those on the Western Front. The troops at the front needed arms and ammunition to fight with, food, clothes and other essential supplies. It was estimated that for every soldier at the front there needed to be three workers in the war industries making the necessary war supplies. Unless the people at home could produce these then the war would be lost. The people at home could not work in the war industries unless they were fed and clothed as well, and all this had to happen while many of the men, including many skilled workers, were out of the country.

The government felt it needed much more power if it was going to organise a major war. Parliament passed the **Defence Of the Realm Act** (DORA) in August 1914 to give the government that power. During the war, when the

Source B

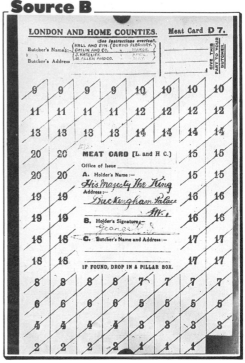

A ration card.

A factory supplying ammunition to the troops.

Source A

government felt it needed extra powers, this act was added to. With its new powers the government could:

- take over the running of the railways;
- nationalise the mines;
- control rents and prices;
- censor the newspapers;
- water down beer so that it was not strong, and cut down pub opening hours;
- even change the time (this was when British Summer Time was introduced).

The key thing for the government was to make sure that industry produced enough. This was a problem as there were fewer workers. Women were keen to help, but neither employers nor the Trade Unions were very happy about this. However, following a major demonstration in London by women with the slogan 'We demand the right to work', the government stepped in and women were not only working in factories, but also in offices where work had traditionally been done by male clerks, and in most major industries. This was a very significant change. Working gave women more freedom and clearly showed that they could do jobs just as well as men.

Industry could only keep producing things if there were raw materials and food for the workers. The Germans tried to starve Britain out of the war by using U Boats (submarines) to sink supply ships on their way to Britain. This nearly worked, and there were major propaganda campaigns to make people eat less and avoid waste. It got to the stage where there was only enough wheat left in the country for one month when Lloyd George introduced the convoy system. This meant that ships waited until there were enough of them to sail with a guard of destroyers. Losses to U Boats went down from 25 per cent to 1 per cent and the crisis was avoided. Rationing eventually had to be introduced as queuing for food was becoming a problem.

Source C

Questions

Section A

1 **a** What were the important jobs which had to be done on the Home Front?
  b Why do you think the government used the phrase 'The Home Front'?

2 Explain how each of the powers the government had under DORA might help win the war.

3 After the war Lloyd George said:

'It would have been utterly impossible for us to have waged a successful war if it had not been for the skill, enthusiasm and industry which the women of this country have thrown into the war.'

  a Why do you think the idea of more women working was not, at first, popular?
  b Why do you think the government eventually insisted that women should be allowed to work in essential industries?

4 Which of the changes that happened on the Home Front during the First World War do you think would be likely to have most effect on Britain after the war?
  Give reasons for your answer.

Section B

5 **a** Source C has no caption. Does this affect its value for a historian?
  b What caption do you think Source C ought to have? Give reasons to explain why you think your caption is a good one.

6 **a** Is there anything unusual about Source B?
  b Does this affect the value of Source B to the historian?

7 Make a table of all the statements in the text which can be supported by sources A, B and C.

8 Find a statement in the text which can be **proved** by one of the sources. Explain why the source proves the statement is true.

9 Is there any difference between a Source **supporting** a statement and a source **proving** a statement? Explain your answer.

11

The Effects of the First World War

In the summer of 1918 American troops were arriving on the Western Front in great numbers, and the Allies began to drive the Germans back. In October, when ordered to sea to attack the British, the German High Seas fleet mutinied. In November the German government negotiated an **armistice** with the Allies, which was agreed and began on 11 November 1918. The fighting in the First World War stopped. However, an armistice is not the same as a peace treaty. It is an agreement to stop fighting while a peace treaty is arranged. The Germans believed they had agreed with the Allies that the peace treaty would be based on a plan for peace called the Fourteen Points published by Woodrow Wilson, the American President. As things turned out they were wrong.

The peace treaty which ended the war with Germany was not negotiated between the Allies and the Germans. Having accepted the armistice the Allies (Britain, France, The United States and Italy) made up the peace treaty themselves and insisted that the German government accept it. This treaty, called the Treaty of Versailles, after the French palace where it was signed, caused much resentment amongst the Germans. The main things the Germans objected to were:

- **the Diktat**   This was the name the Germans gave to the treaty because it was dictated not negotiated. They felt they should have had a say in the decisions. They also felt that some of the terms of the treaty contradicted the Fourteen Points, on which they claimed the peace was to be based.

- **war guilt and reparations**   The Germans were forced to accept that the First World War was their fault. As if this was not bad enough they were also forced to pay **reparations**, money to compensate the Allies for the cost of the war Germany had caused. This figure was fixed at £6,600,000,000.

- **the loss of territory**   German land was taken and given to other countries (see map).

- **disarmament**   The treaty limited the size of the German army and navy, said German troops would never be allowed into the Rhineland, and stopped Germany from having tanks, armoured cars, military aircraft, and submarines.

Source A

War Deaths 1914-18, by country	
Russia	1,750,000
Germany	1,750,000
France	1,500,000
Austria-Hungary	1,250,000
Great Britain	900,000
Italy	600,000
Turkey	300,000
USA	114,000

Source B

Source C

Source D

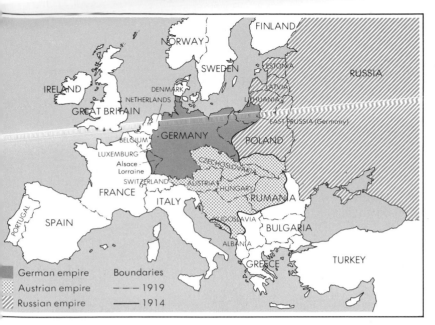

Source F

PEACE AND FUTURE CANNON FODDER

The Tiger: "Curious! I seem to hear a child weeping!"

Source E

A woman's memories of Armistice night in London.

'I left the others and walked slowly up Whitehall, with my heart sinking. All those who I really cared for had gone. For the first time I realized that everything that had made up my life had vanished with Edward and Roland, with Victor and Geoffrey. The War was over; a new age was beginning; but the dead were dead and would never return.'

From Vera Brittain, 'Testament of Youth', 1933.

Questions

Section A

1 Copy out the following sentences re-arranging the 'tails' so that each goes with the right 'head'.

Heads	Tails
a When the German government agreed to an armistice	the leaders of the USA, France, Italy and Britain.
b The Treaty of Versailles was made by Wilson, Clemenceau, Orlando and Lloyd George	to the 'war guilt' clause, reparations, the loss of territory, and to the limitations of the size of their armed forces.
c Because they had no part in drawing up the terms of the treaty	they thought the peace which followed would be based on the Fourteen Points.
d The Germans objected to various parts of the treaty,	the Germans called it a *Diktat*.

2 Draw a graph or pie chart to show the losses sustained by each country during the First World War.

3 Mark on a map the changes made in Europe by the peace treaties after the First World War.

Section B

4 Will Dyson, the cartoonist of Source F, clearly thought the peace treaties would cause trouble in the future.

  a Who are the four men in the cartoon?
  b Why might Dyson have thought the peace treaty would cause trouble?

5 Do you think the peace treaty could have been one of the causes of later trouble in Europe?

6 Do you think the First World War can have been part of the cause of any of the following:

  a Many women being unable to find husbands in the 1920s.
  b The growth of pacifism.
  c Economic problems in the 1920s.
  d The discovery of penicillin in 1928.

Give reasons for your answer in each case.

13

The League of Nations

Activity

What do you think each of these people would have thought about the possibility that there might be another war in Europe, immediately after the end of the First World War?

The setting up of an organisation between countries was one of the main parts of the peace settlement after the First World War. The **Covenant** of the League of Nations, which was its list of rules, was written into each of the peace treaties. The aims of the League were to prevent any further wars and to help solve economic and social problems throughout the world by encouraging co-operation between countries.

The League had eighteen members when it first met in 1920, and its highest ever membership was fifty-nine, so many countries did not join. Even worse, some of the most powerful countries did not join. The first members were those countries which signed the peace treaties at the end of the war plus certain others who were invited to join. Germany was not allowed to join, the USA and Russia did not sign the peace treaties so could not join. This meant three of the great powers were not part of the League. Germany finally joined the League in 1926, but left again in 1934, the same year that Russia joined.

The decisions of the League were made by two bodies, its General Assembly and its Council. The General Assembly (on which all members of the League had one seat) met about once a year. The Council (on which only a few countries including the most powerful had seats), met more often, and could be called at short notice.

As well as these decision-making bodies there were others to do the work. Two major organisations were the Court of International Justice and the International Labour Organisation. The Court dealt with legal arguments between countries. The ILO tried to improve the conditions of the workers in various countries by doing research into what those conditions actually were and encouraging governments to improve them. Both of these parts of the League were quite successful, as were the special commissions set up to deal with particular international problems like Refugees, Slavery or Drugs.

What did not work quite so well was the aim of stopping further wars. During the 1920s the League managed to stop fighting between a number of small countries, but in the

Source A

From the Covenant of the League of Nations

In order to promote international co-operation and to achieve international peace and security
   by the acceptance of obligations not to go to war
   by the prescription of open just and honourable relations between nations
   by the maintainance of justice and a scrupulous respect for all treaties

We agree to this *Covenant of the League of Nations*

Article 16

Should any member of the League fight a war it shall be deemed to have committed an act of war against all other members of the League. They will stop all trade or financial or other relations with the covenant-breaking state.

Source B

The first meeting of the League, 1920.

1930s it was increasingly ignored. Back in 1919 at the peace conference there had been an English plan for the League, that was supported by Woodrow Wilson and accepted, and a French one which was soon forgotten. The French plan gave the League its own army so that it could make sure its decisions would be obeyed, but the British one replaced this with Article 16 (Source A).

As we know, the League did not prevent a second major war within twenty years. It had four main weaknesses. It was too closely linked with the peace treaties which ended the First World War – this made it seem a bit like a club for the winners, and tied it to trying to stop any changes being made to the treaties. It did not have the right members – the USA was never a member, and both Germany and Russia were not members at important times. It had no force of its own to make countries accept its decisions. Finally, it did not get enough support from the two great powers that were members – neither Britain nor France was prepared to go to war to make sure the League was obeyed.

Questions

Section A

1 The League of Nations was rather like a country itself. Think about these institutions in Britain and see if you can think of part of the League that did the same job:

   a the Cabinet
   b Parliament
   c the Civil Service
   d the Courts
   e the police

Write a sentence about each explaining what, if any, part of the League did the same job and why you think it matches up.

2 Which part of the League would deal with the following problems:

   a the heroin trade?
   b an emergency caused because two countries seem about to go to war?
   c a dispute about which country really had legal ownership of an uninhabited island?
   d children being made to work 15-hour days in factories?

3 Which part of the League do you think is meeting in Source B? Give reasons for your answer.

4 Read the last paragraph of the text. Make two lists, one of facts and one of opinions contained in the paragraph.

5 Why do you think the League of Nations failed?

Section B

6 Why do you think people were so determined to set up the League of Nations after the First World War?

7 How do you think a German would feel about the League of Nations?

8 Many historians have said that the reason why the League failed was because it did not have armed forces of its own. The French suggested the League should have armed forces, but other people thought this was a bad idea. Can you explain why many people thought the League should not have armed forces?

9 Copy the following statement into your book:

   'We cannot explain why things happen in history until we know how people were thinking at the time.'

   Do you agree? Explain your answer.

Russia (i): The Causes of the Russian Revolution

Russia was the largest of the great powers in 1914. It was not, however, the strongest. Russia had many problems in 1914; indeed it had been trying to cope with these problems for many years. This section looks at some of these problems and then concentrates on two questions:

- Why was there a revolution?
- Why did the revolution happen when it did?

Facts of geography   Russia covered one sixth of the land surface of the whole world at the start of the twentieth century. Transport between the various parts of Russia could be very slow, and much of the land was more or less uninhabited. There was little industry and most people were peasants who worked on the land. The Trans–Siberian Railway linked the East and West of Russia in 1905, and this encouraged the growth of larger towns and more factories.

Class system   Russian people were divided up into various classes (such as aristocrats, peasants, etc). The division was very rigid and the law even stated that the different classes had to wear certain clothes – almost a uniform.

Condition of the peasants   Most Russians were peasants. They worked on the land for very low pay, and their jobs were hard as there was little use of machines to do heavy work. They lived in very poor conditions and usually did not own any land of their own.

Condition of workers in the towns   Factory work in the towns was fairly new in Russia, and growing. Wages were very low and living conditions were very bad. Often factory workers would have to live in communal houses.

Police state   Russia was ruled by an emperor called the Tsar. The tsars had feared that there might be a rebellion against them and had set up a system of harsh laws and secret police to seek out and crush possible rebels.

Russification   'Russia' contained many areas that had once been independent countries. The tsars decided to stamp out as much of this regional identity as they could in case it led to rebellions.

Rasputin   Rasputin was a monk of the Russian Orthodox Church who became a key adviser to the Tsar (Nicholas) and his family. The Tsar's eldest son suffered from *haemophilia*, a disease that stops blood clotting. Any cut or bruise could

Source A

A Russian political cartoon, 1916.

Rasputin surrounded by his admirers.

Source B

Inside a peasant's house.

Source C

Inside an aristocrat's house.

have been fatal, but Rasputin had the knack of stopping the bleeding, probably by some form of hypnotism. He was disliked by almost everyone, partly because of his drunkenness and partly because of sexual orgies he was involved in which scandalised the court. He became the most important political adviser to the Tsarina (the Tsar's wife) who was left in charge of the government when the Tsar went to the front during the war. Rasputin was murdered by a group of aristocrats in December 1916.

First World War When the war started Russia suffered early defeats. The Russian army never had enough arms or ammunition, and its losses in the fighting were very high. The demands of the war caused major food shortages in the cities, and unrest at how badly the war was being run. The Tsar took over personal charge of the war in August 1915.

The Revolution of March 1917

In January 1917 Lenin, the leader of a Marxist revolutionary group called the Bolsheviks, made a speech in Switzerland where he was in exile. He said he was doubtful whether 'we the old [he was forty-six] would live to see the decisive battles of the coming revolution.'

At the same time a secret police report on the feelings of workers in the Russian capital Petrograd, stated:

'The workers are on the verge of despair, they are quite ready to let themselves go to the wildest excesses of a hunger riot…they assume an openly hostile attitude towards the Government and protest with all means at their disposal at the continuation of the war.'

The secret police were right. Food riots began in Petrograd on 8 March, by 12 March the revolutionaries were in control of Petrograd, and the Tsar resigned on 14 March. There had been a revolution.

Questions

Section A

1 **a** Who do you think the central character in Source A is meant to be? Give reasons for your answer.
   b Who do you think the characters in Source A are meant to be? Give reasons for your answer.
   c What do you think the artist was trying to suggest?

2 Look at Sources B and C. What are the differences between the two houses?

3 During the period before the Revolution in Russia there was a group of richer peasants called *Kulaks*. Do you think the family in Source B were Kulaks? Give reasons for your answer.

Section B

4 Make a table to list the possible causes of the Russian Revolution. Use the following headings:

Cause	Reason why it was a cause	Long or short term	Reason

Fill in the table from the information in this section.

5 Rasputin died in 1916. The Russian Revolution happened in March 1917. Therefore Rasputin cannot have been part of the causes of the Russian Revolution. Do you agree? Give reasons for your answer.

6 The secret police stated that there might be riots in Petrograd because the workers were hungry. There were food riots and these led to the Revolution. Does this mean the only cause we really need to explain the Russian Revolution was the shortage of food in Petrograd? Give reasons for your answer.

Russia (ii): The November Revolution

After the March Revolution power passed from the Tsar to a Provisional Government. This was at first headed by Prince George Lvov; later by Alexander Kerensky, a moderate socialist. The problems which had faced the Tsar's government did not disappear at the March Revolution, and the Provisional Government had many difficult decisions to make.

One of the first decisions it made was to continue with the war. This meant that the problems caused by the war continued, and when a new Russian offensive in June failed, the Provisional Government got the blame for it.

Much of the real power in Russia had to be shared with **soviets**. These were councils elected by groups of workers or

THE IDEAS OF KARL MARX.

He believed history showed that <u>all</u> countries would go through the following changes:

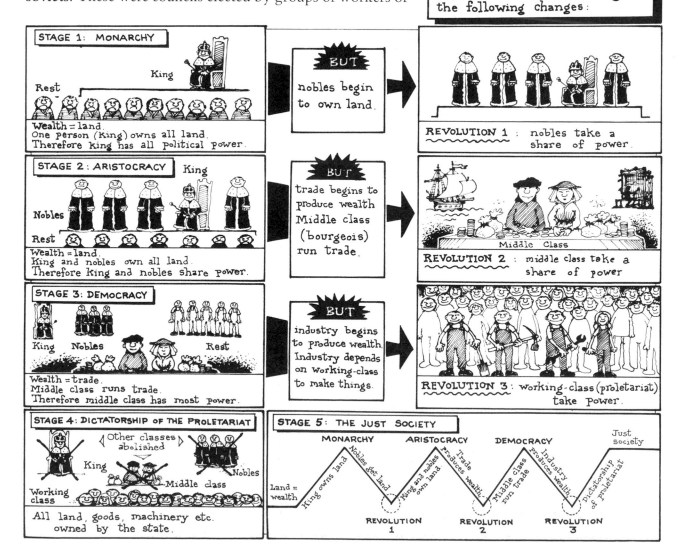

STAGE 1: MONARCHY

King

Rest

Wealth = land.
One person (King) owns all land.
Therefore king has all political power.

BUT nobles begin to own land.

REVOLUTION 1: nobles take a share of power.

STAGE 2: ARISTOCRACY

King

Nobles

Rest

Wealth = land.
King and nobles own all land.
Therefore King and nobles share power.

BUT trade begins to produce wealth. Middle class (bourgeois) run trade.

Middle Class

REVOLUTION 2: middle class take a share of power

STAGE 3: DEMOCRACY

King   Nobles   Rest

Wealth = trade.
Middle class runs trade.
Therefore middle class has most power.

BUT industry begins to produce wealth. Industry depends on working-class to make things.

REVOLUTION 3: working-class (proletariat) take power.

STAGE 4: DICTATORSHIP OF THE PROLETARIAT

Other classes abolished

King

Nobles

Middle class

Working class

All land, goods, machinery etc. owned by the state.

STAGE 5: THE JUST SOCIETY

MONARCHY   ARISTOCRACY   DEMOCRACY   Just society

Land = wealth

King owns land
Nobles get land
King and nobles own land
Trade produces wealth
Middle class run trade
Industry produces wealth
Dictatorship of proletariat

REVOLUTION 1   REVOLUTION 2   REVOLUTION 3

people living in particular places. Local soviets were formed in most areas, and usually contained representatives of workers, peasants and soldiers. The soviet in Petrograd (the capital) was almost as important as the Provisional Government. There was opposition to the Provisional Government in most soviets from people who thought the revolution had not gone far enough. The best organised of these opposition groups were the Bolsheviks, a Marxist group led by Lenin.

The Bolsheviks worked hard to increase their support, helped by the slowness of the Provisional Government in introducing the reforms that people wanted most. The Bolshevik's policy was a simple one, summed up by the slogan:

PEACE, LAND, BREAD.

By the middle of October the Bolsheviks had a majority in the Petrograd soviet, but probably less support in the country as a whole. It seemed to Lenin to be the right time to move against the Provisional Government. On the night of 6 November, Bolshevik soldiers (known as Red Guards) arrested the leaders of the Provisional Government and captured the key buildings in Petrograd. Only Kerensky escaped. The Bolsheviks had succeeded in staging a second revolution within one year. Now Lenin was in power.

Source A

A description of life in Petrograd immediately before the November Revolution, by John Reed, an American journalist who was in Petrograd.

'At night, for economy as well as from fear of air raids, the street lights were few and far between; in private houses the electricity was turned off from six o'clock until midnight. Robberies and housebreaking increased. In apartment houses men took turn at all night guard duty, armed with loaded rifles. This was under the Provisional Government.

Week by week food became scarcer. The daily allowance of bread fell from a pound and a half to a pound, and then three-quarters, half, and a quarter pound. Towards the end there was a week without any bread at all....For milk and bread and sugar and tobacco one had to queue long hours in the chill rain....I have listened in the bread-lines hearing the bitter note of discontent which from time to time burst up through the miraculous good nature of the Russian crowd.

Of course all the theatres were going every night, including Sundays. Karsavina appeared in a new ballet, Chaliapin was singing...

As in all such times the petty conventional life of the city went on, ignoring the Revolution as much as possible.'

Questions

Section A

1 Copy the diagram about the ideas of Karl Marx.

Where in Marx's scheme do you think a Marxist would put the March Revolution? Give reasons for your answer.

2 a Describe a soviet.
b Why do you think the soviet in Petrograd was so important?

3 a What was the Bolshevik's political slogan?
b Do you think these policies would have helped the Bolsheviks win support in the soviets? Explain your answer.

4 Do you think John Reed was a supporter of the Tsar, a supporter of the Provisional Government or a supporter of the Bolsheviks? Give reasons for your answer.

Section B

5 Does Source A help to explain why there was a second revolution in Russia?

6 Karl Marx died in 1883, yet he is often said to have been one of the key figures in the Russian Revolution. How can this be true?

7 Do you think a second revolution in 1917 was inevitable?

Russia (iii): The Fate of the Tsar

The November 1917 Revolution was not well received by the countries still at war with Germany. The Bolsheviks made a separate peace with Germany, which gave the Germans an advantage in the war. There were groups inside Russia which did not accept the Bolshevik government. These groups were called 'White' Russians, while the Bolsheviks and their forces were called the 'Reds'. A civil war began in 1918 between groups of Whites and Lenin's government. At first the Whites seemed to be going well, and in May 1918 White troops were threatening the town of Ekaterinburg, which is where the former Tsar and his family were being kept prisoner by the Bolsheviks. All historians agree that the Tsar (then known by his surname, Romanov) and his family were in Ekaterinburg on 16 July. When Ekaterinburg was captured by the White forces on 25 July they said the Romanovs had been killed. This seems to have been the final straw as far as the governments of Britain, France and the USA were concerned. Troops from all three countries invaded Russia to help the Whites in the civil war. The first were the British who landed on 2 August 1918, even before the First World War was over. The foreign troops were reinforced after the defeat of Germany, but the Reds won the war. It lasted until 1922 and caused even more misery and problems for Russia.

As different sides in the civil war controlled Ekaterinburg, so different investigations were carried out to find out what had happened to the Romanovs.

Source A

Official announcement by the Bolshevik government.

'During the last days Ekaterinburg was seriously threatened by the danger of an advance of White gangs, and at the same time a new plot was discovered, which had the object of snatching out of the hands of the Soviet Government the crowned hangman. In view of these circumstances the leaders of the District Soviet of the Ural decided to execute, by shooting, Nicholas Romanov, which was done on 16 July. The wife and son of Nicholas Romanov have been sent off to a secure place.'

Petrograd Telegraph Agency.

Source B

Report in the 'New York Tribune', December 1918.

[This report describes an interview with the first investigator of the case, Judge Sergeyev, who had supported the March Revolution of 1917, but not the Bolshevik November Revolution.]

'Sergeyev took from his desk a large blue folder and said: "Here I have all the evidence in connection with the Nicholas Romanov case. I examined the lower floor of the building where the royal family lived, and where the crime was supposed to have been committed. I do not believe that all the people were shot there. It is my belief that the Empress, the Tsar's son, and the four other children were not shot in that house. I believe however that the Tsar, his doctor, two servants and the maid were shot in the Ipatiev House.'

Source C

Diagram of the position of people in the murder room according to official witnesses, taken from Judge Sokolov's report.

Source D

Part of a report to the British Government on the disappearance of the Tsar by Sir Charles Eliot, an Englishman who was in Russia at the time.

'Judge Sergeyev, the officer appointed to investigate the crime, showed me over the house.

On the wall opposite the door and on the floor were marks showing where pieces of the wall and floor had been cut out by Sergeyev in order to remove the bullets. The position of the bullets indicated that the victims had been shot while kneeling and that other shots had been fired into them when they had fallen on the floor.

There is no real evidence as to who, or how many, victims there were but it is supposed that there were five, namely the Tsar, Dr Botkin, a maid, and two servants.

On 17 July a train with the blinds down left Ekaterinburg for an unknown destination and it is believed the Empress and the five children were on it.'

Source E

Part of the report of the second official investigator.

[Judge Sergeyev was sacked on 23 January 1919, and replaced by Judge Sokolov on 7 February. The Whites held Ekaterinburg until 14 July 1919 and during that time Sokolov, who had been a supporter of the Tsar, was able to hold his investigations.]

'During the evening of 16 July the seven members of the Romanov family and the four servants with them were still alive.

On 17 July, under cover of darkness, a lorry carried their corpses to the Four Brothers mine. The main purpose was to destroy the bodies. The bodies were chopped into pieces with cutting instruments, destroyed with sulphuric acid, and by burning on bonfires with the aid of petrol. The fatty matter of the corpses melted and spread over the ground where it became mixed with the earth. The murderers threw in the mine objects which had resisted the fire, or which in their haste they had forgotten to burn.'

Source F

'A defector from Communist Poland who was an informant for the CIA said last night that he was Alexi, the only son of Nicholas II, last Tsar of Russia.'

From the 'New York Times', 16 August 1964.

Questions

Section A

1 Who were the Whites and who were the Reds?

2 How did British, French and American troops get involved in a Russian civil war?

3 How do you think this involvement will have affected later Russian views of those countries?

Section B

4 Can you work out approximately when Sir Charles Eliot investigated the case?

5 Does Source A support the conclusion of Judge Sergeyev in Source B? Explain your answer.

6 a Who controlled Ekaterinburg when Sokolov was investigating the case?

   b How would you expect this to affect the reliability of the witnesses Sokolov saw?

7 a Do you think anyone could have escaped from the room as shown in Source C?

   b Does this mean Sokolov's account (Source E) must be reliable? Give reasons for your answer.

8 Does Source F help you to decide whether any of the other sources are reliable or unreliable? Explain your answer.

9 The Bolshevik government soon changed its story and said all the Romanovs had been killed. Why might it have done this?

10 Why might White Russians have wanted people to believe:
   a that the Tsar and all his family had been murdered?
   b that some of the Tsar's family were still alive?

11 What do you think happened to the Romanovs? Give reasons for your answer.

Events 1919–36

The problem which faced the governments of the world in 1920 was how to turn peace into stability. In most countries the war had caused drastic changes in the way people lived. Industry needed to find new things to make, as the demand for arms and ammunition would fall. Women had grown used to new independence during the war, and many did not want to go back to the old ways. The huge armies needed to be cut down to their normal peacetime sizes. In some countries the physical damage of war needed repairing – towns, villages, roads, railways and factories needed rebuilding; and land needed to be made safe for farming. Also there was a general expectation that the sacrifices made during the war demanded that, rather than being returned to its pre-war state, life should be improved. Politicians had talked about creating a 'land fit for heroes' while the war was being fought, and now the heroes wanted something to happen.

In the western world the key problems were created by the economy. The 'land fit for heroes' turned into a land of unemployment and poverty. Most countries did not manage the transition from a war economy to a peace economy very well, and the early 1920s were a time of hardship and unrest as a result. While most countries did eventually sort out these early problems worse was to come. Following the Wall Street Crash of 1929 a depression spread from the United States to Europe. Once again poverty, hunger and the frustration of unemployment were common.

The political developments of these years can very often be seen as the ways various countries dealt with these economic and social problems. In some countries democracy was not strong enough to survive this challenge and it was replaced with dictatorship. Very often this was a right-wing, or Fascist, dictatorship, as in Italy, Germany and Rumania. In these countries individual freedom suffered, the power of trade unions and other political parties was destroyed, and dangerous opponents were often simply killed. Other countries, notably the United States, found ways of solving these problems within the limits of democracy and freedom.

In Russia the communist government was able to survive attacks from anti-communists in Russia and hostile states. Russia too had severe economic problems, and Russia found its solution in a communist dictatorship. While having many ideas directly opposed to the fascist states, Russia, as a dictatorship where individual liberty had almost disappeared, did have some similarities to them. Communism and Fascism were political systems which both offered solutions

to the economic problems of the time, but very different ones. They were seen as opposites, often competing for the same possible supporters. While Fascism was often linked to Nationalism, Communism was seen as an international idea. It was possible for a Communist in a country like Britain to feel loyalty to Russia because Russia was advancing the international communist cause.

Source A

'But they don't necessarily lower their standards by cutting out luxuries and concentrating on necessities; more often it is the other way about – the more natural way, if you come to think if it. Hence the fact that, in a decade of unparalleled depression, the consumption of cheap luxuries has increased. The two things that have probably made the greatest difference of all are the movies and the mass production of cheap smart clothes since the war. The youth who leaves school at fourteen and gets a blind alley job is out of work at twenty, probably for life; but for two pounds ten [£2.50] on the hire-purchase he can buy himself a suit which, for a little while and at a little distance, looks as though it had been tailored in Savile Row. The girl can look like a fashion plate at an even lower price.... At home there is generally a cup of tea going – a "nice cup of tea" – and father, who has been out of work since 1929 is temporarily happy because he has a sure tip for the Cesarewitch.

Trade since the war has had to adjust itself to meet the demands of underpaid, underfed people, with the result that a luxury is almost always cheaper now than a necessity. One pair of plain solid shoes costs as much as two ultra smart pairs. For the price of one square meal you can get two pounds [900 g] of cheap sweets. You can't get much meat for threepence [about 1p], but you can get a lot of fish and chips.... And above all there is gambling, the cheapest of all luxuries. Even people on the verge of starvation can buy a few days hope ("Something to live for", as they call it) by having a penny [about ½p] on a sweepstake.... I happened to be in Yorkshire when Hitler re-occupied the Rhineland. Hitler, Locarno, Fascism, and the threat of war aroused hardly a flicker of interest locally, but the decision of the Football Association to stop publishing their fixtures in advance (this was an attempt to quell the Football Pools) flung all Yorkshire into a storm of fury.... Twenty million people are underfed but literally everyone in England has access to a radio. What we have lost in food we have gained in electricity.

It is quite likely that fish-and-chips, art-silk stockings, tinned salmon, cut price chocolates (five two-ounce [56 g] bars for sixpence [2½p]), the movies, the radio, strong tea, and the Football Pools have between them averted revolution.'

From George Orwell, 'The Road to Wigan Pier', 1937.

Questions

Section A

1 George Orwell, the writer of Source A, was reporting on the conditions of the poor and the unemployed in the North of England. In the passage printed here he offers an explanation why Britain, which suffered as badly as many other countries in the Depression, survived without either a fascist or a communist revolution.

    Do you find his explanation believable?

Section B

One of the things historians try to do when they write history is to create a **synthesis**. This is almost an exercise in pattern making. So much happened in the past that the historian could not describe everything of which there is now evidence. Historians try to produce generalisations which sum up the main features of the time they are writing about. The text of this unit is an example of this. Many things happened between 1919 and 1936, but rather than tell you about as much as can be crammed in, the text tries to pick out some themes that will help you understand the whole period.

2 The photographs in this unit have been carefully chosen to go with the text. Do they fit the themes the text is talking about?

3 Would any three photographs taken during the time do as well?

4 Write your own account of the years 1910–20. See if you can pick out the important themes in those years.

5 Which three pictures in this book would you choose to illustrate your account? Explain why you have chosen each picture.

Russia (iv): Lenin and Stalin

To win the civil war Lenin adopted a series of policies called **War Communism**. He nationalised all factories, stopped trade by individuals rather than the state, and seized all grain from the peasants to share it with soldiers and workers. War Communism was so unpopular that it provoked opposition amongst the peasants, and a serious mutiny in the Red Navy. Lenin replaced it with the **New Economic Policy** in 1921. This allowed the peasants to keep and trade some of their grain, and returned some factories into private hands while others could pay the workers bonuses for higher production.

Lenin died in 1924. Most people had assumed he would be succeeded by Trotsky, who led the Red Army during the civil war. There was some jealousy of Trotsky amongst the other communist leaders though, and this was exploited by Stalin. As Secretary-General of the Communist Party, Stalin could fill all the key jobs in the party with his supporters and, gradually, he came to be the key member of the Politburo. By 1929 he was the undisputed leader of Russia.

Stalin believed that sooner or later the countries of the West would attack Russia because of their hatred of Communism. He said that Russia could not survive such an attack unless it became a developed industrial power like those in the West. His aims were:

1 to greatly expand Russian industry
2 to get money as capital for the new industries
3 to increase agricultural production, partly to feed the increased numbers of workers in the towns, and partly to have a surplus to sell abroad to get the money he needed to set up the new industries.

Stalin used **Five Year Plans** to modernise Russian industry. The plans set targets for the production of key goods, and concentrated on heavy industry. The targets were not always achieved, and were often unrealistically high, but Russian industry did grow in a most remarkable way. Workers were encouraged by bonus payments and by propaganda campaigns. Also they were punished if things went wrong.

Stalin was less successful with agriculture. He wanted to end the small farms owned by the richer peasants called Kulaks; both because they were too small to use machines, and because he thought the Kulaks were enemies of Communism. Stalin's solution was the **collective farm**,

Source A

Sverdlovsk, a new industrial town, in 1928.

Source B

Sverdlovsk in 1933.

Source C

From a speech by Stalin, 1931.
'It is sometimes asked whether it is possible to slow down the tempo a bit, to put a check on the movement. No comrades it is not possible! The tempo must not be reduced. To slacken the pace would mean to lag behind; and those who lag behind are beaten. We do not want to be beaten. Russia was ceaselessly beaten for her backwardness, by Mongol Khans, by Anglo French capitalists, by Japanese barons, she was beaten by all – for her backwardness. For military, cultural, political, industrial, agricultural backwardness. We are fifty or a hundred years behind the advanced countries. We must make good this lag in ten years. Either we do it or they crush us.'

where a large area was owned and farmed jointly. While the landless peasants were happy to join collective farms, the Kulaks, with their own land, were not. Many burned their crops and killed their animals rather than contribute them to the collective farms. Protesters were often shot or sent to labour camps, but the damage done to Russian agriculture was serious. There was a major famine in 1932–3 during which some five million peasants died. By 1937 90 per cent of Russian land had been collectivised. The 1940 grain harvest was 80 per cent higher than in 1913, but meat production did not get back to 1913 levels until 1953. The change brought about an enormous amount of misery, suffering and death in the countryside.

During the 1930s Stalin became worried about opposition to him within Russia. In 1934 he began a series of **purges** against possible opponents. The most famous were given 'show trials' in Moscow, where they almost always confessed to treason against the state, and after which they were either executed or sent to labour camps. All of Lenin's old comrades, the commander of the Red Army, thirteen other generals, and about two-thirds of the officers were executed. About eight million people were put in very harsh labour camps, usually in Siberia, in which many died.

Source D

Industrial production in Russia compared with other great powers in 1940 (in millions of tons)

	Pig iron	Steel	Coal	Electricity (in billion kilowatts)
Russia				
1929	8.0	4.9	40.1	?
1940	14.9	18.4	164.6	39.6
USA	31.9	47.2	395.0	115.9
Britain	6.7	10.3	227.0	30.7
Germany	18.3	22 7	186.0	55.2
France	6.0	6.1	45.5	19.3

From N. Lowe, 'Mastering Modern World History', 1982.

Questions

Section A

1 Copy out these sentences matching up the correct 'tail' to go with each 'head'.

Heads	Tails
a Lenin's policy of War Communism	in the purges many army leaders and old Bolsheviks were killed, about eight million were sent to labour camps.
b Because of the opposition Lenin	modernised industry.
c Stalin was in a strong position to replace Lenin	the creation of collective farms.
d Stalin's policy was based on the belief that	nationalized factories, seized grain, and caused lots of opposition.
e The Five Year Plans	replaced War Communism with the New Economic Policy.
f Agriculture was modernised through	because he could place his supporters in important jobs in the Party.
g All opposition to Stalin was crushed	Russia must one day defend itself against attack from the West.

Section B

2 Explain whether Stalin would have approved of the photographs used on page 24.

3 a Read Source C. What is Stalin suggesting his main aim was?

 b Does the evidence of the Sources suggest Stalin succeeded in this aim?

4 Stalin was right in that Russia was attacked from the West, by Germany, and Russia was able to defeat Germany together with its allies in the Second World War. Was this due to Stalin?

5 Draw up a balance sheet. List on one side the things Stalin did which were good for Russia, and on the other those which were bad for Russia.

6 a Do you agree with either of these epitaphs for Stalin? Give reasons for your answer.
 b Write an epitaph of your own to sum up Stalin's life and explain why you think it is fitting.

The General Strike

The British economy had a short 'boom' at the end of the First World War, with plenty of jobs and high wages. This soon ended, however, and for much of the 1920s unemployment was a problem. The coal industry could not compete with more mechanised industries abroad, and the owners said that the miners would have to take a cut in pay and work more hours.. The miners' union rejected this plan, but, before a strike began, the owners started a 'lock out' (closed the mines themselves). The Trades Union Congress (or TUC which represented all trade unions) backed the miners by calling out workers in other industries to strike in sympathy with them. The workers called out on strike were in the transport, printing, power, building, iron, steel and chemical industries.

This General Strike lasted nine days. National newspapers could not publish normally and both the government and the TUC brought out their own newspapers. While most union members and many other people supported the strike, many people also opposed it, sometimes trying to break it by doing the jobs of striking workers.

Source B

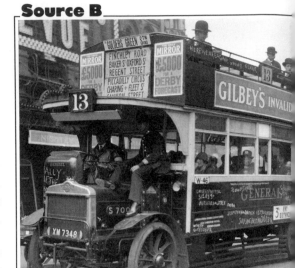

A London bus.

Source A

This photograph was printed in an official history of the TUC with the following caption: An armoured car escorts a food convoy through the streets of London—despite the fact that, from the beginning of the strike, the TUC had made it clear that foodstuffs would be allowed free passage.

Source C

From the autobiography of George Brown, who was later Deputy Leader of the Labour Party.

'My father was a keen trade unionist, he became secretary of the branch. Then came the General Strike. My father brought all the drivers out, then, on the instructions of the TUC he took them back, then he brought them out again... This was because the General Council of the TUC couldn't make up its mind how it wanted to fight the strike, and, indeed, whether it wanted to win or not. But to me it was all wildly exciting and I helped overturn trams driven by blacklegs at the Elephant and Castle. At the end of the strike my father lost his job and he found it hard to get another.'

Source D

HOLD UP OF THE NATION
Government and the Challenge
NO FLINCHING
The Constitution or a Soviet

The general strike is in operation, expressing in no uncertain terms a direct challenge to ordered government.

From 'The British Gazette'.

Source F

'The BBC fully realises the seriousness of its responsibility and will do its best to carry out the responsibility in the most impartial spirit that circumstances will permit. Nothing is more likely to create panic than the complete interruption of genuine news. We will do our best to maintain our tradition of fairness and we ask for fair play in return.'

Statement issued by the BBC, second day of the strike.

Source G

Extracts from the BBC 1pm news bulletin, Friday, 7 May.

'Corporation trams resumed at Yarmouth today.
Southern Railway: Over 500 trains ran yesterday.
300–400 volunteers at Maidstone: half have expressed willingness to be drafted anywhere in England. Large proportion skilled motor drivers. Practically full service of trams.
Halifax: 50 transport workers returned to work. Some textile mills closed for want of coal.
At Pudsey 170 engineers went back yesterday.
North Shields: workers refuse to come out.'

The end of the Strike

The General Council of the TUC was worried by the possible consequences of the General Strike. They were happy to accept a compromise plan even though the government would not promise to accept it. The miners, however, refused to go back to work, sticking to their slogan, 'not a penny off the pay, not a second on the day'. The lock out of the miners lasted another seven months; in the end they had to accept the owners' terms.

Source E

The General Council does not challenge the Constitution.

It is not seeking to substitute unconstitutional government.
Nor is it desirous of undermining our Parliamentary institutions.
The sole aim for the Council is to secure for the miners a decent standard of life.

The Council is engaged in an Industrial dispute.

There is no Constitutional crisis.

From 'The British Worker'.

Questions

Section A

1 Study Source A. What things can you see in the photograph which suggest it was an unusual scene?

2 Why do you think the TUC gave the photograph the caption printed with it?

3 Study Source B. List the unusual things in this photograph and explain why you think each of these things had been done.

4 Study Sources F and G. Does Source G support the BBC's own account of how it was acting during the strike?

Section B

5 Why do you think the government and the TUC issued the statements that they did? (Sources D and E)

6 How do you think George Brown would have felt:
   a if he saw Source A?
   b if he saw Source B?
   c about the BBC's coverage of the strike?

7 Many students volunteered to drive trams, buses and trains. Why do you think this was?

8 How do you think a miner would have felt about the TUC?

USA (i): Boom

In the years immediately after the First World War things seemed to be going well in America. There was hardly any unemployment, so most people had money to spend. There were new and attractive things to buy. **Mass production** meant cars, fridges and radios, which once only the very rich could have bought, could be made cheaply. **Hire purchase** meant people could get these things straight away and pay for them in the coming months or years. As so many things were being bought a large number of workers were employed to make them. These workers in turn had their wages to spend, so they bought more things, so more workers were needed to make the things they bought, … There seemed to be no reason why this prosperity should ever cease.

There was a dark side to America in the '20s though. While most people in the towns and in industry were well off, the farmers and rural workers often suffered great poverty. During the war there had been a market for all the food America could produce, but this was not so as the countries of Europe got back on their feet. **Prohibition** had begun in America in 1920. This was the name given to a law which made it illegal to make, transport or sell any alcoholic drink. Gangsters replaced barkeepers as the people who supplied Americans with drink, and these gangsters often corrupted police and politicians to stay safe themselves. Crime was a big and profitable business. Finally there was the **Ku Klux Klan**. This group of costumed thugs grew in membership immediately after the war, and was responsible for beating up or murdering many it did not agree with – often on racial grounds. It was strongest in the South, and had as many as five million members at one time. The Klan began to interfere in politics as well, but started to lose members when a leader was convicted of rape and murder.

Source A

'Scientific research has demonstrated that alcohol is a poison, it lowers to an appalling degree the character of our citizens, thereby undermining public morals and democracy, [it] produces widespread crime, poverty, and insanity, inflicts disease and untimely death upon hundreds and thousands of citizens, and blights with degeneracy their children unborn.'

From a speech in favour of prohibition given in the Congress.

Source B

Some of the consequences of prohibition.

'In New York, where there had been 15,000 legal saloons, there were soon 32,000 *speakeasies* [places where alcohol was sold illegally].

Al Capone [a Chicago gangster] is generally believed to have been responsible for over 400 murders.

Capone ordered a car which weighed seven tons and sported a steel-visored petrol tank, all round armour plating, windows of one-and-a-half inch thick bullet-proof glass, and an opening window at the back which served as a rear gunner's position. Chicago in 1925, with a population of 3,000,000 had 16,000 more arrests for drunkenness than England and Wales with a population of 40,000,000.

By 1932 2,000 civilians, mainly gangsters and beer-runners, had been killed "in action" and 500 Prohibition agents.'

From Purnell's 'History of the Twentieth Century'.

Source C

The scene after the shooting of Frank Yale, Mafia leader and liquor boss in New York, on the orders of Al Capone.

Source D

The set made for Douglas Fairbanks' film, 'The Thief of Bagdad', 1922.

Source E

Mass production at work: Ford cars outside the factory.

Questions

Section A

1 The economy of the 'Boom' can be thought of as a spiral. Copy the following diagram, adding the labels in the right place, then write a paragraph explaining what it shows.
more workers employed
more goods bought
more goods made
more wages spent

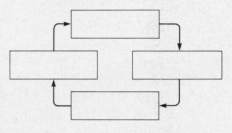

2 What advantages did supporters of prohibition think it would bring America?

3 What do Sources D and E tell you about the economic prosperity of America?

Section B

4 Do Sources D and E help you to explain **why** America became so prosperous in the 1920s?

5 What does Source B suggest were consequences of prohibition?

6 Can speeches in favour of prohibition (such as Source A) be seen as causes of events such as that shown in Source C? Explain your answer.

7 The supporters of prohibition did not want any of the things suggested in Sources B and C to happen.

  a Do you think these things would have happened without prohibition?

  b Does this mean that what people want does not matter in history? Explain your answer.

USA (ii): Roosevelt and the New Deal

The prosperity in America in the 1920s was never equally shared out. Some groups, such as most farmers, had not done well at the height of the Boom. In 1929 there was a stock market 'crash' when the value of stocks and shares fell dramatically. This ruined many rich Americans, and a lack of confidence in the whole economy grew up. People worried that they might not always be so well off, so they saved their money. This meant that industry couldn't sell as much, because people were not sending as much. As industry couldn't sell as much it didn't need to make as much, so it needed fewer workers, so many people lost their jobs. The people who lost their jobs did not have any spare money at all, so there was even less spending. This in turn led to less buying, less being made, and more workers sacked. The 'Boom Spiral' had turned into a 'Bust Spiral'. Things got worse and worse.

There was no unemployment benefit in the United States, and people who lost their jobs lived on the edge of starvation. Many had mortgages to buy their own houses, and when they did not have the money to keep up the payments they were evicted. Banks often had to close because they could not pay back all the money that people had put in their accounts. Some unemployed people, with nowhere else to live, built shanty towns in and around America's great cities. These were called **Hoovervilles** after the President, Herbert Hoover, who did little to end the crisis or to help the poor and homeless. Hoover believed that it was wrong for government to interfere in industry or business, and that the problem would sort itself out if left alone. His answer was that 'prosperity is just around the corner'. Many of the unemployed were not convinced, and a common slogan amongst them was, 'In Hoover we trusted, now we are busted'.

In the 1932 presidential election Hoover's opponent was Franklin D. Roosevelt. Roosevelt was determined to end the Depression, and promised Americans a **New Deal**. He said **relief** from poverty was needed, as was **recovery** of the economy and **reform** to make sure such a slump could not happen again. He easily defeated Hoover and set about restoring Americans' confidence in their country. His policies involved creating jobs for many people by spending a great deal of government money. Unemployed people were offered work on government schemes building airports, schools, roads and dams, or making parks and reservoirs or even acting in government sponsored theatres.

Source A

From one of Roosevelt's speeches during his election campaign, 1932.

'I pledge you, I pledge myself, to a New Deal for the American People. This is more than a political campaign; it is a call to arms. Give me your help, not in votes alone, but to win this crusade to restore America.

I am waging war against Destruction, Deceit and Despair ... With confidence we accept the promise of a New Deal.'

Source B

From one of Roosevelt's speeches during his election campaign, 1932.

'There are two theories of prosperity and of well-being. The first theory is that if we make the rich richer, somehow they will let a part of their prosperity trickle down to the rest of us. The second theory is that if we make the average of mankind comfortable and secure, their prosperity will rise upward.'

Source C

From a radio broadcast made by Roosevelt during the 1936 election.

'In the spring of 1933 we faced a crisis which was the ugly fruit of twelve years' neglect.... Do I need to recall to you the fear of those days – the reports of those who piled supplies in their basements, who laid plans to get their fortunes across the border.... Do I need to recall the law-abiding heads of peaceful families who began to wonder, as they saw their children starve, how they would get the bread they saw in the bakery window?'

Source D

'His voice lent itself remarkably to the radio. It was a natural gift, for in his whole life he never had a lesson in diction or in public speaking. His voice unquestionably helped him to make the people of the country feel that they were an intelligent and understanding part of every government undertaking during his administration.'

Roosevelt's wife talking about him after his death.

Many Americans opposed Roosevelt because he was changing the old American idea that government did not interfere in the economy.

He was easily re-elected in 1936 though (and again in 1940 and 1944), so most must have preferred his ideas to the alternative. He did not, in fact, manage to wipe out unemployment but he was able to create many new jobs, and to improve life for those who still did not get one. Most important of all he managed to restore Americans' confidence in their country. He was very successful in communicating his ideas, using radio to convince people his policies were right, and making speeches which encouraged and convinced Americans.

Source E

THE SOWER.

THE LIFTING DEPRESSION

American newspaper cartoon showing Roosevelt, 1934.

Source F

A Hooverville in Seattle.

Questions

Section A

1 Copy the following diagram which shows the 'slump' spiral, adding the labels in the right place. Write a paragraph to explain what the diagram shows.
fewer workers employed
fewer goods bought
fewer goods made
fewer wages spent

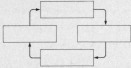

2 Write a paragraph explaining what is meant by: Hoovervilles, the New Deal.

Section B

3 a What was Hoover's policy to deal with the Depression?
b How popular do you think Hoover was?

4 Roosevelt called his radio broadcasts (like Source C) 'fireside chats'. Why do you think he chose this name?

5 Roosevelt said 'We have nothing to fear but fear itself'. Do you think his speeches would have helped Americans regain their confidence in their country?

6 Roosevelt was one of the most important American presidents. Which do you think was the key to his success – his policies or his ability to explain them to people?

Mussolini and Fascist Italy

Although Italy had been on the winning side in the First World War most Italians were not happy with the treatment they got at the end of it. They felt that Italy was not given as much land as it should have been in the peace treaties; they blamed their government for being too weak. Many ex-soldiers were also not happy. Promises made to encourage recruiting during the war were broken, and there was much unemployment. In many areas of Italy 1919 and 1920 were years of considerable unrest. Groups of ex-soldiers took over factories or country estates, and political parties with extreme policies – of both the left and right – grew in power. The Communists organised a general strike in May 1919 but it was a failure. In Milan, communist demonstrators had fought with members of a new right-wing party, the **Fascists**, led by Benito Mussolini. The Fascists took their name from the *fasces*, a bundle of sticks which was the symbol of a judge in Ancient Rome.

The violence of fascist groups, called **Blackshirts** after the uniform they copied from Italy's elite troops in the First World War, became a common feature of Italian politics between 1919 and 1922. They beat up opponents and burned down the buildings of parties or newspapers which disagreed with them. There was little action taken against Fascists for this violence, and many made no attempt to hide their part in it (see Source B).

The Labour Alliance, a socialist organisation, called a general strike in 1922 to protest about the rising level of political violence. The strike failed but Mussolini and the Fascists, who had offered to crush it themselves if the government did not, were able to pose as defenders of Italy. In October 1922 Mussolini felt strong enough to bid for power. He announced a march on Rome by fascist supporters (Source C). Fascist groups occupied public buildings in some northern towns and three columns of them started a 'march' on Rome (mainly by train). Mussolini stayed in Milan. In Rome the government asked the king to proclaim martial law, and had enough loyal soldiers easily to have stopped the Blackshirts. The king at first agreed then refused. Instead he invited Mussolini to become Prime Minister.

When he received the king's offer in a telegram, Mussolini caught the train to Rome and formed a government. The next day the fascist marchers were allowed into Rome on the government's orders and a victory parade was held. This march on Rome became a myth which was fostered by Mussolini. The 30,000 marchers became 300,000; 3000

Source A

'The present government in Italy has failed. We must be ready to take its place. For this reason we are establishing the *Fasci*. The right to the political succession belongs to us because we were the ones who pushed the country into war and led it to victory.'

From a speech by Mussolini at an early fascist meeting.

Source B

'We have set fire to eighty offices of the co-operative societies, and we have destroyed the local socialist headquarters. Every Saturday evening we carry out punitive expeditions. We have the upper hand. The authorities are on our side. They are tired of red flags and socialist insolence.'

From a statement by a fascist in Bologna, 1920.

Source C

Fascists! Italians! The time for determined battle has come! Four years ago the National Army loosed the final offensive which brought it to victory. Today the army of the Blackshirts takes possession of that victory, which has been mutilated. Fascism does not march against the police, but against a political class both cowardly and imbecile, which in four long years has not been able to give a Government to the Nation.'

From Mussolini's proclamation of the march on Rome.

Mussolini the leader in the 'battle for grain', on marshland reclaimed under a government programme. ▶

Source D

Mussolini on horseback.

casualties – 'fascist martyrs' – were invented: Mussolini was painted leading the marchers into Rome on horseback; and the fact that, before they were ordered to let them into Rome the marchers had been stopped by 400 police, was forgotten.

Mussolini's government developed three features. It was a **dictatorship**: that is, Mussolini ruled the country himself, with no real part in decision-making for any parliament. Mussolini always said his government was **active**. New roads were built, major agricultural changes were made, and industry was encouraged. **Violence** still played an important part in fascist politics: opponents were beaten up or murdered, while the fascist thugs were not punished.

Source E

Mussolini and Roman cardinals.

Source F

Fascist slogans: ● 'Believe! Obey! Fight!' ● 'He who has steel has bread!' ● 'Nothing has ever been won in history without bloodshed!' ● 'Better to live one day like a lion than a hundred years like a sheep!' ● 'War is to the male what childbearing is to the female!' ● 'A minute on the battlefield is worth a lifetime of peace!'

Source G

Questions

Section A

1 Describe the situation in Italy at the end of the First World War.

2 Describe the violence that was common in Italian politics in the early 1920s.

3 Describe the way the march on Rome resulted in Mussolini becoming Italy's new leader.

4 Compare Sources A and F. Did Mussolini's Fascism change much between being set up and the time when he was a dictator?

5 Sources D and G were pictures Mussolini was pleased with. What sort of image do you think he wanted to create?

6 **a** What is happening in Source E?
b Why do you think scenes like this were important to Mussolini?

Section B

7 The situation after the First World War, the violent incidents of the early '20s, and the march on Rome could be called **turning-points** in the success of Mussolini. Complete this table which shows the importance of these turning-points.

TURNING-POINT	WHAT HAPPENED	WHAT COULD HAVE HAPPENED
Situation after War	Growth of Fascist party	Growth of Communist and Socialist parties
Violence of Fascists 1919 – 1922		
March on Rome		

8 Copy the following statement into your book. Underline it. Say whether you agree with it or not, and explain why.

Causes in history are the same as causes in science. For any cause there is only one possible result.

Germany (i): The Weimar Republic

Following Germany's defeat in the First World War the Kaiser abdicated and a republic was created. This republic was blamed for accepting the Treaty of Versailles and had to cope with an attempted communist revolution as it came to power. In the republic's early years there were a number of attempts to take over the government by force (called *putsches*). One of these was by Hitler and his new **National Socialist** or **Nazi** party.

As if German prestige had not been hurt enough by defeat in the war, the French occupied an important industrial area, the Ruhr, in January 1923 because the Germans had not kept up with the payment of reparations. This crisis led to a worse one as confidence in German currency collapsed and the country suffered terrible inflation (see Source A). Germany managed to recover from this, helped by American loans, but when the American economy entered the Depression in 1929 the German economy quickly followed. Unemployment rose higher and higher, and many people suffered extreme poverty.

Source A

One loaf of bread cost

 163.15 marks in 1922

 1,512,000 marks in Sept. 1923

250 marks in Jan. 1923

0.63 marks in 1918

3,456 marks in July 1923

201,000, 000,000 marks in Nov. 1923

One egg cost

 1.6 marks in 1921

4,000,000 marks in Sept. 1923

 7 marks in 1922

0.9 marks in 1914

 5,000 marks in July 1923

320,000, 000,000 marks in Nov. 1923

Source B

Miners and their families living in shacks after eviction from their houses in 1931.

Activity

Study Source B and answer the following questions:

1 What things can you see on the roofs of the shacks? Why do you think each was there?
2 What can you tell about the inside of the shacks from this picture?
3 What do you think the advantages and disadvantages of living in these shacks were?

Questions

Section A

1 Describe the problems which the Weimar Republic was faced with.

2 Which of these problems do you think was the greatest? Give reasons for your answer.

Section B

3 How do you think each of the following would have reacted to:
    i the putsches and attempted revolutions
    ii the French occupation of the Ruhr
    iii the inflation of 1923
    iv the unemployment and problems of the Depression?
  a an ex-soldier, disabled during the war and living on a pension
  b a member of the German Communist party
  c the owner of a small grocery shop

4 Do you think the people shown in Source B would have been supporters of the Weimar Rupublic?

5 Hitler and the Nazis offered policies of strong government with much stress on restoring German national prestige. Do you think this was likely to appeal to many people in Germany in the 1920s and '30s? Give reasons for your answer.

(ii): Mein Kampf

In November 1923 the Nazis' attempted putsch in Munich failed. As a result Hitler was sentenced to five years in prison, but was released after only nine months. While he was in prison he was allowed visitors and books. He spent most of the time writing *Mein Kampf*, a statement of his own political views.

Source A

Hitler in prison in 1923. Second from the right is Hess, who was to be Deputy Leader of Nazi Germany.

Extracts from 'Mein Kampf'.

A

When our political meetings first started I ... organised a suitable defensive squad – a squad composed of young men. These young men had been brought up to realise the best form of defence was attack. How these young men did their jobs! Like a swarm of hornets they tackled disturbers at our meetings, regardless of superiority of numbers, however great, indifferent to wounds and bloodshed.

B

A description of a Nazi meeting.

In a few moments the hall was filled with a yelling, shrieking mob. Numerous beermugs flew like shells above the anti-nazi protesters' heads. Amid this uproar one heard the crash of chair legs, the crashing of mugs, groans, yells and screams. It was a mad spectacle. I stood where I was and could observe my boys doing their duty, every one of them ...

C

The people's state must organise its educational work in such a way that the bodies of the young are trained from infancy onwards, so as to be tempered and hardened for the demands made on them in later years. The people's state ought to allow more time for physical training in the school. It is nonsense to burden young brains with a load of material of which they will retain only a small part. Not a day should be allowed to pass in which the young pupil does not have one hour of physical training in the morning and one in the evening: every kind of sport and gymnastics should be included, especially boxing ...

D

Special importance (in girls' education) must be given to physical training, and only after that must the importance of mental training be taken into account. In the education of a girl the final goal always to be kept in mind is that she will one day be a mother.

Questions

For each question explain your answers, giving the best reasons you can.

1. Do you think Hitler was in favour of violence as a means of winning political power?

2. *Mein Kampf* was written while Hitler was in prison. Can you suggest a reason why he would not mind showing the Nazis to be violent, even though this might mean trouble with the law?

3. How does Hitler's attitude to education compare with modern ones?

4. Why do you think Hitler was so keen on:
   a boxing for boys
   b motherhood for girls?

5. Would you say Hitler's stay in prison was harsh?

6. Hitler's Germany was a **totalitarian** country (that is, one where the state controlled every aspect of life). Was Hitler hoping to be a totalitarian leader when he wrote *Mein Kampf*?

7. '*Mein Kampf* shows that Hitler was determined to start a war, and that his policies were aimed at getting Germany ready for it.'
   Do you agree with this statement?

35

Germany (iii): Hitler's Germany

The Nazi party had few seats in the **Reichstag** (the German Parliament) during the relatively prosperous 1920s. When the Depression started, however, support for the Nazis grew; they went from 12 seats (1928) to 107 (1930), to 230 (July 1932). They lost some support during 1932, only winning 196 seats in a second election in November. This still meant that the Nazis were a large party (there were 608 seats altogether), and that Hitler was an important politician. The Nazis had used the normal methods of politicians; speeches, rallies, marches, posters, and books and newspaper stories. They had also used violence and intimidation. They had two private armies, the SA and the SS, whose members wore uniforms, were paid, and would do whatever the leaders felt was necessary.

Hitler did not actually come to power through violence, however. He was invited to become chancellor by President Hindenburg, who had dismissed the previous chancellor. This was the normal way that chancellors were appointed under the constitution of the Weimar Republic. Once in power, Hitler lost no time in making sure he stayed there. A new election was called for March 1933, Hitler drafted nearly 50,000 SA and SS men into the police, and all the power of the State was used to support the Nazi candidates. Opposition meetings were broken up and their supporters and candidates attacked. In this election the Nazis won 44 per cent of the votes, which did not give them a majority of seats in the Reichstag. Hitler found an excuse to suspend the constitution. The Reichstag building had been burned down, and the Nazis blamed the Communists and said this was the start of a major attack on Germany. Hitler proposed the **Enabling Law** which stated he could govern for four years without the approval of the Reichstag. This was accepted by the newly elected Reichstag on 23 March 1933.

The state that Hitler created was a **totalitarian** one. It controlled almost all aspects of life, using its secret police, the **Gestapo**, to make sure people obeyed. All other political parties were banned; local government was largely in the hands of Nazi Special Commissioners appointed by the central government in Berlin; the civil service was purged of people the Nazis did not like; trade unions were abolished; education was controlled; youth organisations were set up which boys and girls **had** to join; the economy was organised; the churches were bullied and eventually a Nazi church set up; there was even a list of banned books, plays,

Source A

I have just returned from Germany. I have now seen the famous German leader and also something of the great change he has made. Whatever one may think of his methods – and they are certainly not those of a parliamentary country – there can be no doubt he has achieved a marvellous change in the spirit of the people, in their attitude to each other, and in their economic and social outlook. One man accomplished this miracle. A born leader of men, the national Leader. He is also securing them against the constant dread of starvation, which is one of the worst memories of the last years of war and the first years of peace.'

Lloyd George, former British Prime Minister, in the 'Daily Express', November 1936.

Source B

A man was taken to Nazi barracks where he was stripped, beaten and tortured with steel rods for three hours. At intervals he was forced to wipe up the blood from the floor with his clothes. When he became unconscious the Nazis wrenched open his mouth with such force that part of his lip was torn away, and poured acid down his throat. He was flung, a bleeding mass, into the street where his wife was anxiously waiting for news of him. He was just able to tell her what happened to him. When his wife wiped away the froth from his lips her handerchief was corroded by the strong acid which had been poured into him. He died some hours later in agonizing pain. The official diagnosis gave apoplexy as the cause of death.'

Walter Citrine, Secretary of the TUC, in a TUC/Labour Party pamphlet, 'Hitlerism', 1933.

films and music. As well as intimidating people to accept his ideas, Hitler also tried to convince them. The Propaganda Ministry, headed by Dr Goebbels, controlled newspapers, radio and films. It also organised mass rallies, such as the ones held at Nuremburg every year, to show the power of Nazi Germany.

During their rise to power the Nazis had gained some support by being anti-Jewish. This continued as part of their **Racial Policy**. They taught that the Germans were **Aryans**, a race destined to dominate the world. It was important that the race should not become 'adulterated' with that of 'slave' races. They also blamed the Jews for most of Germany's problems (including the loss of the First World War and the Depression). In 1934 the SA led a boycott of Jewish shops, which soon had to be marked with a yellow star or the word 'JUDEN'. Segregated seating for Jews was introduced on public transport. In 1935 the **Nuremburg Laws** took away Jews' rights to vote and to marry non-Jews. Violence against Jews increased and usually went unpunished.

Source C

Cartoon published in the 'Evening Standard', March 1933.

Source D

A Nazi badge; the words read, 'He who buys from a Jew is a traitor to his people'.

Questions

Section A

1 Copy out the following paragraph, choosing one of the alternatives printed in italics each time.

   The Nazi party did *better/worse* when the Depression caused unemployment in Germany. They used many methods to win support including violence as well as *legal/illegal* means. Hitler *did/did not* come to power legally. He *called/banned* elections and drafted many *SA and SS/unemployed* into the police. After the Reichstag building was burned down *Hitler/President Hindenburg* proposed the Enabling Law which made him a dictator for four years.

2 What do we mean if we call a government 'totalitarian'?

3 Which things done by the Nazis suggest they were a totalitarian government? In each case say why you think the policy was a totalitarian one.

Section B

4 What do you think the aim of the artist of Source C was?

5 What do you think the aim of the designer of Source D was?

6 What impression of Hitler and his Germany do you get from:

   a Source A
   b Source B
   c Source C

7 How can you explain this difference in impression?

8 Is there any difference between Sources A–C and Source D for a historian studying Nazi Germany?

9 Which of the sources do you think a historian studying Nazi Germany would find most reliable?

China (i): Revolution and Warlords

China had been bullied by the western powers and Japan in the years before the First World War. The Chinese government had lost much respect in the eyes of its people as a result of this. A revolution in 1911 brought down the last of the emperors, but no new government strong enough to control all of China emerged. Instead **warlords**, local rulers backed by their own troops, controlled most of China. Only the area around Canton remained in the hands of the **Kuomintang**, the Nationalist People's Party. Law and order had broken down, and for the peasants, the majority of the population, life must have seemed worse than under the emperors.

In the late 1920s, in alliance with the Chinese Communist party, the Kuomintang (KMT) was able to defeat most of the warlords and reunify much of the country. In 1927, however, the KMT turned on its communist allies and massacred thousands in the cities. In 1928 the campaign against the warlords was over, and the KMT was internationally recognised as the government of China. By 1930 it was strong enough to begin a series of attacks aimed at destroying the remaining Communists in the Kiangsi province. But the Communists survived—thanks to the Long March, a 6000-mile fighting retreat that took them right across China.

Source A

A street execution in a warlord's capital.

Source B

'The village was a place of deep destitution and dire want. Here were some 400 souls, all members of the Hsio clan, living in their old joint families both large and small. Of these only two families were well-to-do, and they kept themselves apart and above their destitute kin. They owned almost all the land in and about the village, renting it to their poorer relatives, who cultivated it as tenants, giving up 50 per cent of the crop as rent. More – it was not merely half their hard-earned harvests that went to the owners, but there were the gifts that had to be made to keep in the good graces of the wealthy relatives. To the kitchen doors of the two big families came tenants bearing chickens, eggs, fruit, and woven baskets. In bad times they came offering their daughters for sale, and the entire staff of servants of the two big families consisted of women slaves bought in this way from the poor of the village.'

Agnes Smedley, 'Chinese Destinies', 1934.

Source C

A marching song of the Red Army

'You are poor,
Of ten men, nine are poor
If the nine poor men unite
Where then are the tiger landlords?'

Source D

Rules for the behaviour of soldiers in the communist Red Army.

1 Speak politely.
2 Pay fairly for what you buy.
3 Return everything you borrow.
4 Pay for anything you damage.
5 Don't hit or swear at people.
6 Don't damage crops.
7 Don't take liberties with women.
8 Don't ill-treat prisoners.

Source E

Coolies.

Source F

Peasant ploughing.

Source G

'We stood on the hillside at Lunmen. Eight soldiers of the Sixty-eighth Division had been sent with us as bodyguards. We all stood together on the hillside and gazed at the rolling fields beyond, in which peasant men and women were working, bending over their hoes. The soldiers watched, and one of them said to the others: "I'll bet I'm a better shot than you."

To prove his boast, he raised his gun to his shoulder and fired at the figures of the peasants. The dust spurted up – he had missed. The other soldiers laughed at his bad marksmanship. Then one by one they raised their guns and tried their luck, using the peasants as targets. The peasants ran hither and thither in terror, and we thought of chickens or birds. The soldiers laughed as they fired, watching the comical antics of their victims. Finally two of them came up to us, offered their rifles, and asked us to try our luck. We were foreigners. They wanted to see if foreigners were better shots than Chinese.'

Agnes Smedley, a European journalist in China, reporting the experiences of two friends she believed were truthful.

Questions

Section A

1 Draw a time-line to show the events mentioned in the text. How closely can you link each of the sources to this time-line?

2 Is there enough evidence in Sources A and F to justify the suggestion that Chinese cities were developed but the countryside was backward?

3 Using all the sources and the text, make a list of at least five major problems facing China at this time. Write a sentence or two to describe each problem.

4 Working with one other person, compare your lists and make up a new list which has six problems facing China, with the problems listed in order of importance.

5 Working with another group of two, compare your lists. Agree a new list which has the three problems you think any Chinese government should have tried to tackle first, with some suggestions as to what might have been done.

Section B

6 How do you react to: **a** Source A? **b** Source E? **c** Source G?

7 How would you expect a Chinese peasant of the time to react to: **a** Source A? **b** Source E? **c** Source G?

8 How would you expect a Chinese landlord of the time to react to: **a** Source A? **b** Source E? **c** Source G?

9 How would you expect a Chinese warlord of the time to react to: **a** Source A? **b** Source E? **c** Source G?

10 How would you expect a Chinese Communist of the time to react to: **a** Source A? **b** Source E? **c** Source G?

11 Why are your answers to questions 6–10 different?

12 Why is this difference important to historians?

Events 1931–9

The story of international relations in the 1930s can be seen as the failure of the system created after the First World War to preserve the world from further war. The League of Nations had already been seen to be dangerously weak; it was shown in the 1930s to be unable to do the job it was created for.

There were a number of countries which, for various reasons, had aggressive foreign policies during the 1930s. These countries either actively wanted to start wars, or were quite happy to risk a war to get what they wanted. This increase in warlike feelings was seen as being linked with the growth of Fascist and other undemocratic political systems. Some people saw the growth of Fascism in so many countries as a threat to the future of all democracies. They felt the world needed a crusade to save it from Fascism. Others, including many Fascists and those prepared to support them, saw the growth of Communism as the great threat to the future. Many people in many countries supported either Communism or Fascism simply because they saw it as the best answer to the threat of the other movement.

The first sizeable war was the Japanese invasion of Manchuria in 1931. The League was quite unable to stop this war, although this was just the sort of crisis it was designed to deal with. Japan simply left the League and ignored the words of condemnation which League members uttered. The Japanese were the first nation to show that noble speeches, unless backed with force, could not stop a war.

While fighting never really stopped after 1931 in the East, the West had a few more years of peace. One of the solutions to unemployment was to increase the size of a country's armed forces and to build more and newer weapons. International attempts to get countries to agree on a policy of disarmament failed, and the language of politicians became much more aggressive in many countries.

Italy next demonstrated the failure of the League as a peacekeeping force by its 1935 invasion of Ethiopia. Again fine words did not stop a war. Nor did they stop the civil war which broke out in Spain in 1936, nor the series of aggressive moves by which Hitler expanded German power between 1936 and 1939. To add to this, the Japanese extended their operations in China and from 1937 onwards invaded much of the Chinese mainland.

During the late 1930s the world was clearly not at peace. The question was whether the various wars would involve great powers in fighting each other, rather than picking on smaller countries. The British and French governments worked particularly hard to avoid this, by a policy known as 'appeasement'. This tried to avoid a major war by giving the aggressive powers, especially Hitler's Germany, what they wanted. All the time Germany, Italy or Japan were alone they could not risk war against another great power because they could not hope to defeat the strength of all the other powers should they unite against them. Germany, Italy and Japan were allied by the end of 1937, but this did not really make them strong enough to be safe. The alliance which probably finished all hopes of peace between the Great Powers was the Nazi-Soviet Non Aggression Pact. In this pact, signed in August 1939, Russia and Germany agreed not to fight one another for at least ten years. Hitler invaded Poland, which led directly to war with Britain and France, while Russia invaded Finland and occupied part of Poland 'for protection'.

Questions

1 Draw a time-line from 1931-9 which shows the events mentioned in this unit.

2 We usually say the Second World War began in 1939, but some countries chose other dates.

 a What date do you think the Second World War started? Give reasons for your answer.
 b When, if at all, did the Second World War become inevitable? Give reasons for your answer.

3 The cartoons on the opposite page were drawn by David Low, who worked for the *London Evening Standard* throughout these years. They were published between 1934 and 1939.
 Write a list of them in chronological order, and explain why you have chosen to put them in the order you have chosen.

4 Write a short paragraph to go with each of the cartoons so that the six cartoons, plus the six paragraphs, give a short account of the years 1934-9.

Source A

MASS MURDER IN CHINA.

Source B

PROGRESS OF MAN. 1935 A.D.

Source C

I'M BRINGING PEACE TO THE
POOR SUFFERING BASQUES

Source D

THE CONFERENCE EXCUSES ITSELF.

Source E

THE MAN WHO TOOK THE LID OFF.

Source F

RENDEZVOUS

41

Events 1939-45

When war broke out in 1939, Poland was quickly defeated. The war in the West developed so slowly, and with such a lack of significant fighting, that it was called the 'phoney war'.

In the spring of 1940 the Germans had captured, in quick succession, Denmark, Norway, the Netherlands and Belgium. The British army in France was nearly cut off, and was lucky to escape capture by a mass evacuation from Dunkirk. France itself surrendered soon after Dunkirk, and was divided in two: a German-occupied area, and Vichy France – part of the South ruled by a government acceptable to the Germans.

Hitler believed the British would see there was no future in the war and make a peace leaving him master of the continent. Britain would have nothing to do with this idea, and so Hitler was stopped from having a short war with a quick victory. His plans to invade Britain were based on the need to control the skies. German defeat in the Battle of Britain prevented an invasion in 1940.

Hitler turned his attention to Russia. On 22 June 1941 he broke the Nazi–Soviet Non Aggression Pact and began a massive invasion. Much Russian territory was captured in the early months of the war; and terrible atrocities were committed by the Nazis in the captured areas. However, Russia is a large country and the Russians were able to hold the German advance.

The United States had been a passive supporter of Britain at the start of the war, providing war-materials, although at a price. It entered the war when the Japanese, looking to expand their power still further in the Pacific, attacked the American fleet at Pearl Harbor. While there was no necessary link between this Pacific War and the one going on in Europe, Roosevelt saw that there was a long-term connection, and the United States declared war on Germany as well as Japan in 1941.

The successes of the Axis Powers (as Germany, Italy, Japan and their lesser allies were known) gradually stopped. The German defeat at El Alamein started an allied advance which liberated North Africa, and continued with invasions of Sicily and Italy. In Russia the cream of the German army was defeated and, with heavy losses, forced back on the long retreat which was to finish in Berlin. Finally, in the Pacific the string of Japanese successes were stopped, the Japanese navy was beaten at Midway, and the slow reconquest of captured islands begun. While the Russians pushed the Germans back across Eastern Europe, the British and Americans invaded France and attacked Germany from the West. The war in Europe ended with the Russians having liberated eastern Europe, while the British and Americans had liberated western Europe. This distinction remained important as each of the Allies created new states in its own image.

Atomic weapons were used before Japan surrendered and so two of the main concerns of our time – the split of the world into Communist and Non-Communist blocs, and the danger of nuclear war – both grew out of the last stage of the fighting of the Second World War.

Questions

1 Draw a time-line which shows all the events mentioned in the text. The exact dates can be worked out by using the information in the maps.

2 Using your time-line and the maps, divide up the Second World War into a number of periods. How many periods will you need? What are the turning-points where one period ends and another begins? Give reasons for your answers.

3 Was there a single turning-point in the war when the Allies' victory became the most likely outcome? Explain your answer.

4 Do you think the general trends in the war you were looking for in the last two questions would have been apparent to people at the time? Give reasons for your answer.

5 A historian has suggested that in the defeat of the Axis powers the contribution of the British was time, that of the Russians was men, and that of the Americans was resources. Do you agree?

Map 1

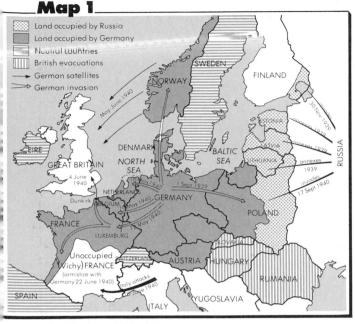

Legend:
- Land occupied by Russia
- Land occupied by Germany
- Neutral countries
- British evacuations
- German satellites
- German invasion

Blitzkrieg, 1939–40.

Map 3

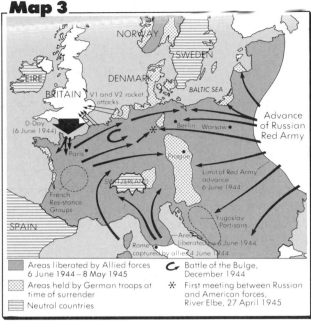

- Areas liberated by Allied forces 6 June 1944 – 8 May 1945
- Areas held by German troops at time of surrender
- Neutral countries
- Battle of the Bulge, December 1944
- First meeting between Russian and American forces, River Elbe, 27 April 1945

The defeat of Germany, 1944–5.

Map 2

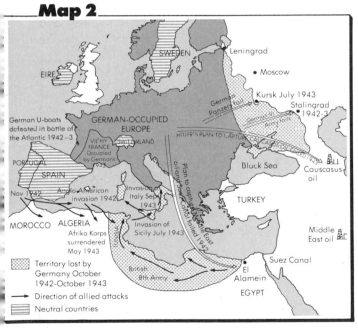

- Territory lost by Germany October 1942-October 1943
- Direction of allied attacks
- Neutral countries

Turning-points, 1942–3.

Map 4

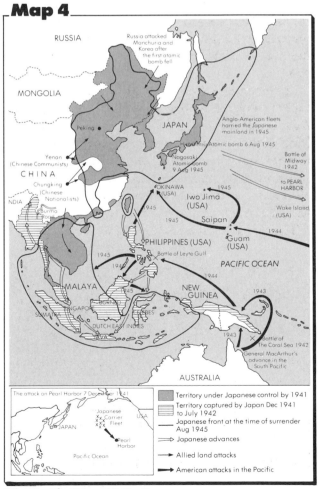

The attack on Pearl Harbor 7 December 1941

- Territory under Japanese control by 1941
- Territory captured by Japan Dec 1941 to July 1942
- Japanese front at the time of surrender Aug 1945
- Japanese advances
- Allied land attacks
- American attacks in the Pacific

The Pacific War, 1941–5.

43

The Japanese Invasion of Manchuria

The first real test of the League of Nation's ability to preserve peace came in 1931 when Japan invaded Manchuria, a province of China. The Japanese claimed Chinese troops had provoked the attack by sabotaging a Japanese railway line. The Chinese denied this and the League eventually sent a Commission to Manchuria to look into the truth of the claim. The Commission said it could find no evidence to support the Japanese story and the League eventually ordered the Japanese to withdraw from Manchuria and return the province to China. By this time it was 1933 and the Japanese refused. They simply resigned from the League of Nations.

A China's Weakness

China was a weak country still split by internal wars. The KMT government was concentrating on destroying the Chinese Communists, and anyway the Chinese army was nowhere near as strong as the Japanese one.

B Japan's Economic Crisis of 1922

Japan had prospered during the First World War as it was able to fill the gap left by European firms which made only war materials. By the end of the war Japan's cotton exports had trebled and its merchant navy doubled. By 1921 this trade boom was over, as markets lost to European countries again. There was also a 'farm crisis' as the price of rice dropped. There was much unemployment and the government was blamed for the problems.

Source A

'Uneasy Street' – David Low cartoon, 9 January 1933.

The expansion of Japan to 1936.

C Manchuria Attractive

Manchuria had important raw materials which Japan was short of – coal and iron. It also had a large population who could become a market for the goods the Japanese were no longer able to sell.

D Democracy Unpopular

The government was not popular with many conservative groups in Japan, which also did not really value the idea of democracy itself. Old habits of obedience to the Emperor and to a strong government were common, especially amongst the army.

E The Depression

The world depression of 1929 affected Japan badly. Its export trade was badly hit, especially the vital silk export trade. Over a half of Japanese factories were closed down, and the farmers who had relied on the money made from silk were also in trouble.

F Military Pressure

There was a group of military leaders who despised the government and wished to take over running Japan themselves. They felt they were not quite strong enough to do this in 1931, but that if they started and won a foreign war they would become more popular. Also Japan would be doing the sort of thing they believed it should do.

Questions

Section A

1 Does the map help explain why Manchuria was an attractive target for the Japanese?

2 Do you think the Chinese should have been surprised by the Japanese attack?

3 **a** Who are the figures in top hats in the cartoon supposed to be?
   b Why do you think the cartoonist has chosen to draw this scene to represent the invasion of Manchuria?
   c Do you think the cartoonist approves of the policy of governments like his own over the invasion?

4 Does the cartoon suggest:

   a most people in Britain supported the invasion;
   b most people in Britain were against the invasion;
   c neither of these?

   Give reasons for your answer.

Section B

5 Each of the boxes in this unit contains some information about a possible cause of the invasion of Manchuria. The boxes have been arranged in a random order.
   The following diagrams use the letter of each box as a label. i.e.

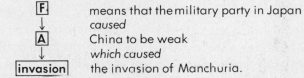

F means that the military party in Japan *caused* A China to be weak *which caused* invasion the invasion of Manchuria.

   Do you think this is right? Explain your answer?

6 These two causes could be put together in other ways:

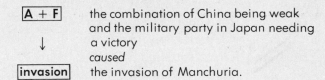

A + F the combination of China being weak and the military party in Japan needing a victory *caused* invasion the invasion of Manchuria.

   Why is this a better explanation than the diagram in question 5?

7 Copy the following diagram, explain what it means, and say whether you think it is correct or not.

D
↓
C
↓
invasion

8 Copy the following diagram, explain what it means, and say whether you think it is correct or not.

B
↓
D
↓
invasion

9 Draw your own diagram to show how you think the causes worked together. Most historians would include all six boxes as causes of the invasion.

The Spanish Civil War

Spain was a monarchy with a parliamentary government in the 1920s but, following much unrest, the King abdicated in 1931. The new republican government was popular with some Spanish people but not with others. In 1936 there was a revolt against the government by a part of the army backed by the Spanish Fascist party (the **Falange**). This revolt, led by General Franco, soon developed into a full scale civil war. In some of the areas controlled by the government, power was shared with communist and anarchist leaders.

This war was seen as a possible threat to European peace. Britain and France set up a **Non-intervention Committee**, which was to make sure no European power got involved. Many people in European countries thought that a fascist takeover in Spain would make a fascist takeover of all Europe more likely, and they wished to help the Spanish government against the Fascists. So many men from other countries volunteered to fight that the Spanish government formed the **International Brigade**, which included many Communists. Russia also began to offer weapons and other supplies to the Spanish government. The fascist states saw Franco and his forces (who called themselves **Nationalists**) as their natural allies. Hitler, while claiming to accept the Non-Intervention Committee, sent crack troops and planes to Spain. He said they were volunteers. They were called the Condor Legion and are thought to have given Hitler and his leaders a chance to try out many of their military ideas. Mussolini also sent Italian troops to help Franco.

The war was an increasingly bitter struggle. Franco and the Nationalists, partly because of the superiority of their German and Italian supplied weapons, were able to crush slowly the republic's defences. By 1939 Franco had won the war and ruled Spain.

The bombing of Guernica

Guernica was in the Basque region famous for its historic and religious importance. During the civil war it was attacked and captured by the Nationalists. Guernica was almost totally destroyed during the campaign. Republicans said it was bombed and machine-gunned by planes from the Condor Legion. This was the first real example of mass bombing of a civilian target, and it caused much outrage around the world. The Nationalists denied the bombing story and said the town had been blown up and burned by retreating republican troops. The sources in this unit look at these two claims.

Source A

'I did learn something about the famous Guernica controversy through my friendship with a British and French journalist who entered the town with the first Nationalist troops to occupy it, and who closely examined the damage and questioned many of the inhabitants. This was the communists' most successful single propaganda coup of the war, and it created a myth which has passed into history. According to this myth Guernica was razed by German Stukas as an experiment in dive bombing. The truth is that the town, an important communications centre and divisional HQ, was bombed by the Nationalist air force – not the German – who hit the railway station and an arms factory: later it was dynamited and set on fire by retreating republicans.'

Peter Kemp, a soldier who fought on Franco's side in the civil war, writing in 1976.

Source B

Though thirty-eight years had elapsed, in 1975 the Franco regime was still refusing to co-operate with any impartial inquiry into the event.

Guernica's mayor suggested we leave as soon as he learned of our presence.

The secretary of the Parliament Building [in Guernica] became even more hostile when he learned of our visit. "On instructions from Madrid," he refused us facilities, and his assistant, Charo Zubelalia, the twenty-year-old daughter of a Spanish officer, told us that the police could make our life "difficult" if we continued to ask questions.'

Gordon Thomas's and Max Morgan-Witts's account of their visit to Guernica to research their book, 'The Day Guernica Died'.

Source C

'I walked through the still-burning town. Hundreds of bodies had been found in the debris. Most were charred beyond recognition. At least two hundred others were riddled with machine-gun bullets as they fled to the hills.'

'Daily Express', April 1937.

Source D

Photograph of German bombers approaching Guernica which the local priest, Father Arrontegui, said he took.

Source E

'Juan Guezureya saw two HE-51s swoop on the market place. To Juan it seemed as if their guns "systematically raked the whole area. The two planes just flew back and forth at about one hundred feet, like flying sheep dogs rounding up people for the slaughter."

Nobody had time to identify or count the total number of bodies. Later, it was estimated that close to fifty people received injuries during this particular strafing.'

From Gordon Thomas and Max Morgan-Witts, 'The Day Guernica Died', based on their conversation with Juan Guezureya, an eyewitness of the events in Guernica.

Source F

The remains of the centre of Guernica.

Questions

Evidence

Section A

1 What started the Spanish Civil War?

2 Draw up a table with two columns, headed 'Republicans' and 'Nationalists'. Read through the text and add each group or country mentioned to the correct side of the table.

3 a What was the aim of the Non-Intervention Committee?
  b Do you think the Non-Intervention Committee succeeded?

Section B

4 What does Source C say had happened to Guernica?

5 Do you think the journalist mentioned in Source A was the one who wrote Source C?

6 What does Source A say happened to Guernica?

7 Does Source F support or contradict Source A?

8 Does Source C contradict Source A?

9 Does Source D **prove** that Guernica was bombed by the Fascists, not damaged by the Republicans?

10 How reliable do you think the following would be for a historian trying to find out what happened in Guernica?

   a Source A
   b Source E

11 Does Source B help you to decide what happened in Guernica?

12 What do you think happened to Guernica? Give reasons for your answer.

Appeasement

public opinion(!?)

During the 1930s there were a number of crises which seemed to threaten world peace. Some were wars, like the invasion of Manchuria or the Spanish Civil War. The danger was that these wars would spread until they became a new world war. Other crises did not quite come to fighting but there was always a danger that they would.

March 1935 – Hitler introduced conscription in Germany The Treaty of Versailles had limited the size of Germany's forces. Conscription (forcing people of a certain age to join the forces) meant this part of the Versailles settlement would be broken.

June 1935 – Anglo-German Naval Agreement France, Britain and Italy protested at conscription in Germany. The force of this protest was lost, however, when Britain signed a separate agreement with Germany about the sizes of the two countries' navies. This accepted that the Germans would build submarines, which was also forbidden by the Versailles treaty.

October 1935 – invasion of Ethiopia Mussolini ordered an Italian invasion of Ethiopia. Haile Selassie, the Emperor of Ethiopia, appealed to the League of Nations for help but the League could do nothing to stop the invasion.

March 1936 – German occupation of the Rhineland The Rhineland was the area of Germany on the border with France. By the Treaty of Versailles it was to be demilitarised (no troops or fortifications allowed). Hitler ordered the German army back into this area. His troops had secret orders that if the French objected they were to retreat, because the French still had a more powerful army. However, neither Britain nor France made a significant protest.

October 1936 – Rome–Berlin Axis Mussolini had at first been unsure about Hitler but the events of 1935 and 1936 convinced him that Hitler would be a more successful ally than Britain and France.

March 1938 – Anschluss Hitler had been born in Austria, a German-speaking country, which he had long wanted to make part of Germany. His chance came when Austrian Nazis, demonstrating for union with Germany, caused the Austrian government to hold a referendum asking the Austrian people whether they wanted union (*Anschluss*) or not. Hitler sent troops in, organised a referendum himself, and got a high yes vote.

Source A

[Mass Observation was the name of a group who made a series of studies of public opinion and ordinary people's way of life during the 1930s. They made a number of surveys of public opinion during the September 1938 crisis. Their surveys included statistics and interviews.]

Selections from Mass Observation interviews in September 1938.

'**Woman of 40:** "Things will be a lot better now, thank God. Chamberlain's done it for once, hasn't he? This'll stop it."

Man of 45: "He's done the right thing. He tried to mediate and that was what was wanted by everybody. Who wants a bloody war? Let 'em fight it if they do."

Man of 70: "I think he's doing wrong. He should have gone to Czechoslovakia first. I think he's got no right to go to Munich and the rest of the Government should give him a good hiding. I'm an old soldier. Why shouldn't the Czechs fight for their country? Why should we allow a bully like Hitler to dominate Europe. Let's fight him and finish with it."'

Source B

Crowd outside 10 Downing Street, after Chamberlain's final return from Munich. Chamberlain and his wife are at the window above the door.

Source C

'*Stepping Stones to Glory*' – David Low cartoon, 8 July 1936.

Source D

"Why should we take a stand about someone pushing someone else when its all so far away.."

'*Increasing Pressure*' – David Low cartoon, 18 February 1938.

Source E

'*Nightmare Waiting List*' – David Low cartoon, 9 September 1938.

September 1938 – Czechoslovakia and the Munich Crisis
Hitler next demanded that the German-speaking parts of Czechoslovakia should be given to Germany. The Czech government refused, and it seemed war might break out. In Britain gas masks were issued and trenches dug as air-raid precautions. Chamberlain, the Prime Minister, flew three times to Munich and reached an agreement with Hitler which, he said, guaranteed 'peace in our time'. However, the cost of this agreement was that Hitler took the areas he wanted in Czechoslovakia.

Questions

Section A

1 Make a table in your books with the following headings:
CRISIS; DATE; COUNTRY CAUSING PROBLEM; DESCRIPTION OF PROBLEM; RESULT; CONSEQUENCES.
The first entry might read: German conscription; March 1935; Germany; Forces increased in size which was against terms of Versailles treaty; Britain, France and Italy protested but nothing done to stop Germans; Hitler saw he could break Treaty, might do it again, and German forces would get strong enough to fight another war.

2 The word 'appeasement' is something used to describe the policies of countries like Britain and France during the 1930s. It means to pacify someone by giving them what they want. Write a sentence about each crisis saying whether or not you think it shows appeasement in action.

3 a What was the cartoonist Low predicting would happen in Source C?
  b Whose hand is pulling the lever in Source D and what does the soldier represent?
  c What was Low predicting Hitler would do after the Austrian crisis in Source D?
  d What crisis was happening when Low drew Source E?
  e What did Low predict would happen after the September 1938 crisis?

4 Do you think Low changed his ideas about Hitler much?

5 Did Low agree with the appeasement policies followed by western governments?

Section B

6 Study the following list of problems:
  a Fear of the damage which another world war would cause.
  b Fear of a fascist takeover of the world.
  c Fear of losing a war with Germany because Britain's forces were not strong enough.
  Which of these do you think the British government thought was the greatest danger? Give reasons for your answer.

7 Source B shows the crowd outside 10 Downing Street the night Chamberlain returned from Munich. How do you think they felt about the solution to the crisis?

8 Source A gives the reaction of three Londoners to the Munich crisis of 1938. Which do you think would have been the most common reaction? Give reasons for your answer.

25

Britain's War 1939–42

In 1939 Hitler demanded territory from Poland. This time Britain and France said they would stand by the Poles if Germany attacked. Hitler, perhaps convinced by the events of the previous few years that they would not, invaded when the Poles refused to give him the land. The Germans entered Poland on 1 September 1939 and on 3 September 1939 Britain and France declared war on Germany. They were not able to do much for the Poles, however, as Hitler's army, using its new tactic of **Blitzkrieg**, quickly conquered the country. *Blitzkrieg* (German for 'lightning war') involved a very fast war with attacks by aircraft and tanks.

In England the start of the war had been marked by great activity. Air-raid precautions were taken seriously and thousands of children evacuated from the cities to villages where it was thought there would be less chance of bombing. However, there was a period when little seemed to happen, called the 'phoney war'. Many people thought the government was not doing enough to win the war. These fears seemed justified when Hitler invaded Norway and conquered it within twenty-one days. Partly as a consequence of this, Chamberlain's government fell and was replaced by a National Government–a coalition of Labour and Conservative ministers headed by Winston Churchill. The fall of Norway was quickly followed by German victories over Holland, Belgium and France. The British army was trapped at the Channel port of Dunkirk. Just as it seemed the whole army must surrender, an evacuation was attempted. The navy, together with just about every boat in the south of England capable of crossing the Channel, brought back over 338,000 troops. Most of their equipment was lost but the soldiers would be able to fight again. Although Dunkirk was the last stage of a major defeat for the British Army, Churchill turned it into a propaganda weapon, concentrating on the miraculous rescue of the troops and talking about the 'Dunkirk Spirit' which would overcome all odds.

The German invasion of Britain was planned by Hitler (see Source F). The first stage was to defeat the RAF and control the skies over Britain; this was the **Battle of Britain**. To start with the **Luftwaffe** (German airforce) concentrated on destroying British airfields; in September this policy was switched to one of bombing London. Having failed to beat the RAF Luftwaffe planes could only attack at night when they were harder to shoot down. Bombing cities was intended to break the morale of the British and make them want peace at almost any price. While it did cause much damage and hardship, and over 250,000 casualties, it failed in its main aim. If anything the Blitz made people more determined that Nazi Germany should be destroyed.

Questions

Section A

1 What was **Blitzkrieg**?

2 What was the 'phoney war'?

3 Why did the Chamberlain government fall in Britain?

4 Which countries was **Blitzkrieg** used against in 1940?

5 Which English government do you think is referred to in Source B?

6 What effect do you think Churchill's speeches would have on his listeners?

Section B

Oral history is the name historians give to work based on evidence taken from conversation with people who lived through the events being studied. The people, or at least their memories, are the primary sources. Obviously this technique can only be used about events in the recent past. The Second World War can still be studied in this way, especially the events on the Home Front.

Historians need to find people to talk to, and to have a good idea of what questions to ask them. To complete this exercise you will have to do some research yourself and talk to someone who can remember something of the war.

Before you talk to the person work out a list of questions. It might help to use some of the sources in this section as starting points. While you are talking you will need to either note down your subject's answers or, if you can, tape-record the conversation.

7 Describe what you found out about life during the Second World War from your interview.

8 What advantages do you think oral history has for a historian?

9 What disadvantages do you think oral history has for a historian?

Source A

'All Behind You, Winston' – David Low cartoon, 14 May 1940.

Source B

'Peashooters' – David Low cartoon, 10 May 1940.

Source C

CHURCHMAN'S CIGARETTES

REMOVAL OF INCENDIARY BOMB WITH SCOOP AND HOE

A cigarette card from a series on air-raid precautions.

Source D

'Even though large tracts of Europe have fallen into the grip of the Gestapo and Nazi rule, we shall not flag or fail. We shall go on to the end. We shall fight in France, we shall fight in the seas and the oceans, we shall fight with growing confidence and growing strength in the air; we shall defend our island, whatever the cost may be. We shall fight on the beaches; we shall fight on the landing grounds, we shall fight in the fields and in the streets, we shall fight in the hills; we shall never surrender.'

From a speech by Churchill.

Source E

'Hitler knows he will have to break us in this island or lose the war. If we can stand up to him all Europe may be free and the life of the world may move forward into broad, sunlit uplands. But if we fail, then the whole world ... will sink into the abyss of a new dark age. Let us therefore brace ourselves to our duties, and so bear ourselves that, if the British Empire and its commonwealth last for a thousand years, men will still say: "This was their finest hour".'

From a speech by Churchill.

Source F

'DIRECTIVE NUMBER 16

Since England, in spite of her helpless military situation, shows no sign of being ready to come to an understanding, I have decided to prepare an invasion operation against England, and if necessary, carry it out. The aim of this operation will be to occupy the English homeland completely.

... Preparations must be completed by the middle of August. These preparations must create such conditions as will make a landing in England possible.

(a) The English Air Force must be so reduced that it is unable to deliver any significant attack against the German crossing.'

Part of Hitler's directive ordering the preparations for the invasion of England.

Source G

An underground station, one night during the Blitz.

26

Why Did Hitler Invade Russia?

The Nazi–Soviet Non-Aggression Pact of 1939 had come as a great surprise, or even shock, to many people. Safe from attack by Russia, Hitler had been able to invade Poland, while Stalin had tried to protect Russia by invading Finland and occupying eastern Poland. Trade had increased between the two countries while Hitler's war aims seemed concentrated in the West.

This did not last, however, and on 22 June 1941 Germany began an invasion of Russia. The Russians were not properly prepared for this attack – despite being given the details by a spy, and being warned by allied governments that it was likely. Stalin believed, in the short-term at least, he could trust Hitler. He was wrong.

Today Russia is one of the two great super-powers. For another country to declare war on it seems almost unthinkable, yet Hitler did. This unit is largely concerned with explaining just how such a decision could be made. Over a hundred years before, Napoleon, then Emperor of France, had conquered most of Europe except Britain. Just like Hitler, Napoleon had decided to leave the British enemy in the West, and to destroy the danger from Russia in the East. Napoleon failed. His army got as far as capturing Moscow but it was trapped by the Russian winter. Napoleon did not recover from this defeat, which is usually seen as the turning-point in the Napoleonic wars. Clearly Hitler must have felt that he could succeed where Napoleon had not.

Source A

'Someone is Taking Someone for a Walk'–David Low cartoon, 2 November 1939.

Source B

'DIRECTIVE 21

The German Armed Forces must be prepared, even before the conclusion of the war against England, to crush Soviet Russia in a rapid campaign.

… I shall issue orders for the deployment against Soviet Russia eight weeks before the operation is timed to begin. Preparations which require more time than this will be put in hand now and will be concluded by 15 May 1941.

It is of decisive importance that our intention to attack should not be known.'

Hitler's Directive to the German Forces, dated 18 December 1940.

Source C

From an article describing relations between Russia and Germany 1939–41.

'Soviet supplies to Germany were speeded up. Two hundred thousand tons of grain were delivered in April, and five million promised for the coming year – far more than the Germans later got from conquered Russia. Rubber from the Far East was rushed through Soviet Russia by special trains until the very day war broke out.'

A.J.P. Taylor, 'The False Alliance'.

Activities

1 Who are the two characters in the cartoon (Source A)?

2 What event do you think the cartoon is commenting on?

3 What did Low think would happen in the end?

Source D

DIRECTIVE 32

After the destruction of the Soviet Armed Forces, Germany and Italy will be military masters of the European continent. No serious threat to Europe will then remain. The defence of this area, and foreseeable future offensive action, will require considerably smaller forces than have been required hitherto. The main efforts of the armaments industry can be diverted to the navy and the air force.... The newly conquered territories in the East must be organized, made secure, and, in full co-operation with the Armed Forces, exploited economically.'

Hitler's Directive to the German Forces, 11 June 1941.

Source E

From a radio broadcast by Stalin 11 days after the German attack on Russia.

'Fascist Germany suddenly and treacherously broke the non-aggression pact which she had concluded in 1939 with the USSR. It may be asked how could the Soviet Government have consented to conclude a non-aggression pact with such perfidious people, such fiends as Hitler and Ribbentrop? Was this not an error on the part of the Soviet Government? Of course not! Non-aggression pacts are pacts of peace between two states. It was such a pact that Germany proposed to us in 1939. Could the Soviet Government have declined such a proposal? I think not a single peace-loving state could decline a peace treaty with a neighbouring state even though the latter was headed by such monsters and cannibals as Hitler and Ribbentrop.'

Lebensraum

This was the name given to Hitler's policy of expansion for Germany. The word literally means 'living room' in German. Hitler felt that his Germany would need room to expand in the East. Territory captured in this area could be lived in by the expanding German population, and the raw materials could be used to make Germany stronger. Any expansion of Germany to the East would bring it into conflict with Russia, either because the land Hitler was hoping to take was Russian, or because the Russians would not feel safe with a stronger Germany as their neighbour.

Questions

Section A

1 What happened as a result of the Nazi – Soviet Non-Aggression Pact?

2 When did Hitler give the order to start planning the attack on Russia, and when was the attack actually started?

3 What evidence is there to suggest that Russia was not prepared for this attack?

4 Do you think Stalin was right to defend the Nazi – Soviet Non-Aggression Pact as a good idea (Source E)?

Section B

5 a What was *Lebensraum*?
  b Did this give Hitler any reason for an attack on Russia?

6 a What changes was Hitler planning in Directive 32?
  b What evidence is there to show that Hitler was confident of beating Russia?

7 In a directive issued before the fighting with Russia actually began Hitler ordered that the SS would have 'special tasks' in conquered Russia because of the need to 'settle the conflict between two opposite political systems'.
  Could this have been one of Hitler's aims in starting the invasion?

8 On the evidence of these sources which man started the war between Russia and Germany?

9 Do you agree with this statement? 'Hitler invaded Russia because he thought Russia would be easy to beat, he could stamp out Communism, cut down the size of his army, and get new territory for Germany in the East.'

10 The results of the war were the weakening of Germany, the invasion of Germany by Russia, and the defeat of the German army. Does this mean Hitler cannot have been the one who wanted to start it?

27

Why Did the Japanese Attack Pearl Harbor?

In December 1941 Japan, with a population of about 70 million, attacked the United States – at the time the world's greatest industrial power. At first glance this seems at least as strange as the German decision to attack Russia. How could such a small country have believed it could, in the end, beat such a powerful one? This unit looks at the causes of the Japanese decision to attack the USA. The Japanese government was not stupid. From its point of view in 1941 an attack on the United States was the best policy. In the boxes which follow are a series of factors which may help to explain this decision. Can you work out why it seemed such a good idea to the Japanese?

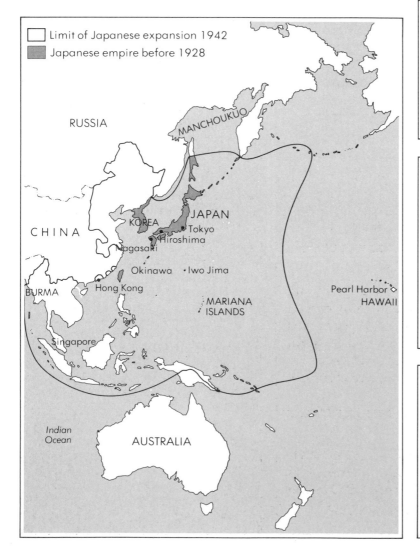

Limit of Japanese expansion 1942
Japanese empire before 1928

A

In the middle of the nineteenth century Japan had been a 'backward' country which had had nothing like the industrial revolution of the West. This meant Japan could not stand up to countries like the USA and Britain. The Japanese started a policy of modernisation with the aim of making themselves as powerful as any other major power. By 1905 they were strong enough to defeat Russia, and to take part in the First World War, but more growth would be needed if they were to equal the front rank powers.

B

Democracy was not highly thought of by many Japanese. Most thought that the generals were more honourable than the politicians.

C

By a treaty signed in 1923 Japan was to stay inferior to Britain and the United States in naval power. The treaty said the Japanese could only build three ships for every five built by Britain and by the United States.

D

The population growth in Japan was so great that when the depression of the 1930s reached Japan there was a real danger of mass starvation. Population growth also meant that the country was overcrowded.

E

The invasion of Manchuria was seen as a success. The League of Nations protested but could do nothing. Food and raw materials could be taken back to Japan and Japanese goods could be sold there. Chinese territory came to be seen as the logical place for Japan to expand. Military leaders were seen as the ones who had secured this victory for the Japanese people.

F

In 1937 Japan invaded China. Rapid conquests were made. The League of Nations again protested.

G

The United States was the great power most concerned with the Pacific. In 1938 the American government asked its industries to put a 'moral embargo' on Japan and not to sell it any aircraft or other 'engines of war'. In fact the only important things Japan bought from America were oil, petrol and scrap iron, none of which was covered. The Japanese people were told that America was a land of unemployment and gangsters which could not be expected to defeat a nation as patriotic and hardworking as the Japanese.

H

Japan was determined to extend its territory and influence further, and announced the formation of the Greater East Asia Co-Prosperity Sphere which really meant that Japan intended to control South East Asia and the Pacific. The Americans objected and banned all trade with Japan.

I

Japanese admirals believed any war between Japan and America would be decided at sea. If they waited their stocks of oil would run down. If they attacked and destroyed the United States' fleet in Pearl Harbor (Hawaii) it would take America at least a year to put another fleet to sea. During this time Japan could have conquered territory with all the resources it needed.

J

The Japanese attacked Pearl Harbor on 7 December 1941. The Americans were not prepared and some damage was done. However, the main part of the fleet had sailed out on exercises some days before and so was not damaged.

Questions

Section A

1. Write a paragraph to explain why Japan attacked Pearl Harbor. Use the information given in each of the boxes by writing a sentence about each one and then a second sentence saying how that factor helped cause the war.

Section B

2. Is it true to say that the Japanese attack on Pearl Harbor had more than one cause? Explain your answer.

3. Causes can be divided up into different types. An **enabling** cause is one that is needed to allow something to happen. It does not mean a particular event *will* happen, but that event *could not* happen unless the enabling cause had happened first. Suggest which of the causes of the Japanese attack on Pearl Harbor was an enabling cause, and explain why.

4. Describe examples of the following types of cause and explain why they are examples of that type of cause.
   a an economic cause
   b a geographical or physical cause

5. Does chance play an important part in human events? Give reasons for your answer.

28

The Secret War

I n almost all wars soldiers have tried to find out what the enemy was doing and have tried to mislead the enemy about what they were doing themselves. In the Second World War both sides had their successes in this 'secret war', but the successes of the Allies were perhaps the most important.

Information, or intelligence, about the enemy had to come from somewhere – usually called its source. All intelligence needed to be evaluated as well. Some of it might not be true, and might have been planted deliberately to mislead. One of the most important ways of evaluating intelligence was to see just where it had come from and to check whether it was genuine. A historian would call this establishing the source's **provenance** and the whole process of intelligence work was rather like the work of a historian. Indeed some of Britain's best intelligence officers during the war were historians.

Source A

'Hitler had ordered Rommel to face Montgomery at the Mareth line. Rommel planned to swing back from Kasserine south-eastward to the Mareth line and there ambush Montgomery's advance guard before the main body of 8 Army could reach it. Montgomery's forces were strung out and Rommel hoped to deal him a blow which would send him reeling back towards Egypt. Rommel explained his intentions to Kesselring over the water in Rome [by use of the Enigma code machine]. Within hours Bletchley Park [the British de-coding centre] had read his plan and sent it to Montgomery. Ordered into full speed ahead Montgomery's main army arrived next morning in time to defeat Rommel, who left Africa two days later never to return.'

From Peter Calvocoressi, 'Top Secret Ultra'. Calvocoressi worked in the British decoding team at Bletchley Park.

Source B

Lydda airfield, Palestine, before camouflage.

Source C

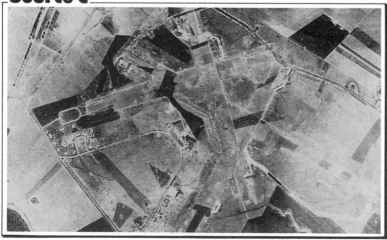

Lydda airfield after camouflage. The runways have been painted and other parts of the site ploughed to blend in with the local countryside.

This unit looks in depth at one example of the main types of intelligence work: deceiving the enemy and finding out what the enemy was doing. The Germans felt their radio messages were safe from interception because they were turned into code by a complicated machine called Enigma. The message was typed on an Enigma machine and turned into meaningless groups of letters. These letters were then sent by Morse code, and when they were typed into another Enigma machine they produced the original message. British intelligence officers were able to decode many of these messages at a special centre in Bletchley Park. The decoded messages, called 'Ultra' by the British, could be trusted as they were the secret internal communications of the Germans, who had no idea the Enigma codes had been broken.

Source D

'The idea was that the dead body of an officer should be taken in a submarine to the coast of Spain and there floated off at a time when the tide would wash it ashore. In the pocket of his tunic there would be a letter from one of our war chiefs to General Alexander, in which would be given a false objective for Operation Husky. We hoped the Spaniards would assume the body was from an aircraft which had been shot down and, as they were pro-German, that they would pass on the letter to the German mission in Madrid.

To get the body of a man who had not obviously died of some disease or as a result of being smashed up in some accident, and who had no relatives who would wish to attend his funeral, can have been no easy task, but somehow we got hold of a suitable corpse which had been a Captain of Royal Marines. He had, I think, died of a heart attack and we were a little worried that when the body was washed up the Spaniards would realize that he had not been drowned, so would suspect a trick. But that had to be risked.

Although the letter was on Cabinet Office paper it appeared to be only a private letter sent from one friend to another; the passage that mattered being just a casual reference to coming events of which the two generals had common knowledge, inserted between passages of gossip. With this in the dead man's pocket, we put several forged hotel bills and private letters purporting to come from a girl. The body was then tinned and delivered to the commander of a submarine.

In due course the Spaniards correctly notified the nearest British Consul that the body of one of our officers had been washed up, and handed to him all the papers that had been on it. It was disappointing to learn on their arrival that the letter had not been opened. But MI6 sent it to their laboratory for special examination, and it transpired that it had been skilfully opened, then re-sealed.'

From Denis Wheatley, 'The Deception Planners: My Secret War'. Wheatley was involved in planning operations to mislead the Germans from 1941 to 1945.

Questions

Section A

1 How had the British got the information about Rommel's plans in Source A?

2 How useful do you think the information about Rommel's plans was to Montgomery?

3 Study Sources B and C. Such deception tactics obviously took considerable time and trouble. Why do you think the Allies thought they were worth it?

4 What was the point of the operation described in Source D?

Section B

5 How could the British be sure of the reliability of the information in Source A?

6 What steps did the British take to give their false story in Source D a believable provenance?

7 How could the British have improved the provenance of their information?

8 In what ways was the work of a war-time intelligence officer similar to that of a historian?

29

The Holocaust

Source A

'He had already identified "Ivan" as Mr John Demjanjuk, the defendant, who has been charged with crimes against humanity. ....
When he was asked how close he had been to "Ivan" in the camp, the floodgates burst.

"I saw 'Ivan' every day at all hours. I rubbed shoulders with him almost as part of my work. He was there all the time by the gas chambers, gouging out eyes, cutting off a girl's breast then standing back and enjoying his handiwork. He was looking with such enjoyment at the crushed skulls and the crushed faces. He was looking as if he had done a tremendously good job. I can't find a word in the human language to compare him to. It was from another planet."

He also described how Ivan had hacked at the corpses, cutting open the bellies of pregnant women.

"A man's healthy brain can't grasp what went on. It is not of this planet. Killing women, killing children. Why? I ask myself. Why? It is because we were Jews." '

From a report of the trial of John Demjanjuk in 'The Times', 25 February 1987. The witness giving evidence was Pinchas Epstein, a survivor of the Treblinka Concentration Camp.

62 – 65

Source B

'Mr Rosenberg described how he had volunteered to do "light work" the day after arriving at the death camp, still unaware of what went on there. With a group of others he was marched off to the extermination area.

"I saw a mountain of corpses," he said. Among them must have been his mother and three sisters who had arrived at the camp with him. "We started retreating but we were beaten to work by a German whip. We were lashed. They said: 'Get the stretchers: grab a corpse and run.' " They had to run and dump bodies in a huge burial pit and then "gallop like a horse" back to get another. ....

In the depth of winter, new orders arrived to burn all the bodies. "Everything had frozen from the cold. We had to hack our way through the corpses with pickaxes in order to make it possible for the excavator to pull out a pile of them." '

From the evidence of Eliyahu Rosenberg in 'The Times', 26 February 1987.

Source C

'I've Settled the Fate of the Jews – and of Germans' – David Low cartoon, 14 December 1942.

Source D

'Not All Guilty' – David Low cartoon, 19 April 1945.

Source E

'Since 1942 enormous transports of Jews have come to Auschwitz. A very small number have been sent to the labour camp, while an average of 90 per cent have been taken from the train and killed.

The Crematorium contains a large hall, a gas chamber, and a furnace. People are assembled in a hall which contains 2000 and gives the impression of a swimming bath. They have to undress and are given a piece of soap and a towel as if they are going to the baths. Then they are crowded into a gas chamber which is sealed. SS men in gas masks then pour in the poison gas. At the end of three minutes all the bodies are dead. The dead bodies are taken away in carts to the furnace to be burnt.'

From a summary of intelligence reports from Czechoslovakia in the British Foreign Office Archives, dated 1944.

Sources A and B were the testimony of witnesses in a trial in 1987. In many ways the historian's use of a source is similar to the use of evidence in a trial, each is one of a number of things used to find out the truth. Historians often talk about their **evidence**, by which they mean using part of a source to support or contradict an idea about the past. You will probably already know something about the **Holocaust**, Hitler's 'final solution' to his 'Jewish problem'. This unit provides you with some sources that you can use as evidence to discover some of the things that happened. The outrage felt by people as news of the Holocaust became known has led to many of those involved in running the concentration camps (such as the guard being tried in Sources A and B) being tried for crimes against humanity. These people often argue in defence that the Holocaust didn't happen, and it is all Jewish propaganda, or that they are not the same person as the one involved in the concentration camp. The sources here will give you evidence to decide whether the first defence is true.

Source F

'I was ordered to establish extermination facilities at Auschwitz. I visited Treblinka [another Concentration Camp] to find out how they carried out exterminations. The commandant told me he had liquified 80,000 in one half year. He used carbon monoxide gas and I didn't think his methods were very efficient. So I used Cyclon B. It took from three to fifteen minutes to kill people. We knew when they were dead because their screaming stopped. After the bodies were removed, our special commandoes took off the rings and extracted the gold from the teeth of the corpses. Another improvement we made over Treblinka was that we built our gas-chambers to take 2000 people at one time.'

Source G

Source H

'The hiring out of concentration camp inmates to industry gives a daily return of 6 to 8 marks of which 70 pfennigs must be deducted for food and clothing. Assuming a camp inmate's life expectation of nine months the profit is 1431 marks. This can be increased by the rational use of the corpse, i.e. by means of gold fillings, clothing, valuables, etc. But on the other hand every corpse represents a loss of 2 marks, which is the cost of cremation.'

From the notes of an SS officer in the concentration camps.

From the evidence of Rudolf Hoess, Commandant of Auschwitz, at the Nuremberg War Crimes Trial.

Questions

Section A

1 What was the Holocaust?

2 When did it happen?

3 What happened?

4 What connection, if any, do you think the following had with the Holocaust:

   a Hitler's view of the Jews?
   b the Second World War?
   c developments in industrial and scientific techniques?

5 How did other countries react when they found out what was happening in the concentration camps?

Section B

6 If you were to say, 'Source G shows a lot of bodies' you have used the source to get information. If you say 'Source G shows that **large numbers of people were killed in concentration camps**, *because the photograph was taken in a concentration camp and there are so many bodies they need mass graves to bury them*,' you have done a lot more. You have used the source as **evidence** to support a statement about the past, and *explained why you think the source is reliable evidence for the statement you have made.*

   a From your answers to the questions in Section A find an example where you used a source as evidence and explain how you were using it as evidence.
   b Is the historian's use of evidence similar to the use of evidence in courts? Explain your answer.

30

Hiroshima

Germany surrendered unconditionally on 7 May 1945, but the Japanese chose to fight on alone. After their initial successes in the Pacific war the Japanese had been steadily pushed back. There was no indication, however, that Japan was ready to surrender. The Japanese code of behaviour valued self-sacrifice and suicide rather than failure. Each small island recaptured in the Pacific was defended desperately: 4000 Americans died capturing Iwo Jima and 12,000 at Okinawa. The same spirit could be seen in the Kamikaze pilots who deliberately crashed their planes, loaded with explosives, into American battleships. The cost in lives of an invasion of the Japanese mainland worried both generals and politicians.

Scientists, however, were just about ready to provide an alternative. Throughout the war scientists from both sides had been racing to make the first atomic bomb. The Americans tested the first bomb on 16 July 1945. It worked. Truman, the new American President, had to decide whether to use the bomb against the Japanese or not. He demanded Japanese surrender and, when that didn't come, two atomic bombs were dropped: at Hiroshima on 6 August and at Nagasaki three days later. The Japanese surrendered, though historians cannot agree whether this was due to the general hopelessness of their situation or because of the bombs.

Source A

Japanese tank trap: soldier and bomb set to explode together.

Source B

'I thought an airplane must have crashed into the sun. Over Mount Kamahura the biggest thing I ever saw, the biggest thing there ever was, was sticking right up into the sky. It kept getting taller and taller all the time and wider and wider. After a few minutes I saw something coming up the road that looked like a parade of roast chickens. I would rather blind myself than ever have to see such a sight again.'

Makota Nagai, aged 10, Nagasaki.

Source C

'The hour was early; the morning still, warm, and beautiful. Clad in vest and pants, I was sprawled on the living room floor exhausted because I had spent a sleepless night on duty as an air-raid warden in my hospital.

Suddenly, a strong flash of light startled me – and then another. Garden shadows disappeared. The view where a moment before all had been so bright and sunny was now dark and hazy. Through swirling dust I could barely see a wooden column that had supported a corner of my house. It was leaning crazily and the roof sagged dangerously. To my surprise I discovered that I was completely naked. How odd! Where were my vest and pants? What had happened? All over the right side of my body I was cut and bleeding. A large splinter was protruding from a mangled wound in my thigh, and something warm trickled into my mouth. My cheek was torn. Embedded in my neck was a sizable fragment of glass which I matter-of-factly took out, and with the detachment of one stunned and shocked I studied it and my bloodstained hand.

[He found his wife and they went into the street.] A house across from us began to sway and then fell almost at our feet. Our own house began to sway, and in a minute it, too, collapsed in a cloud of dust. Other buildings caved in or toppled. Fires sprang up and whipped by a vicious wind began to spread .... There were the shadowy forms of people, some of whom looked like walking ghosts. Others moved as though in pain, like scarecrows, their arms held out from their bodies. These people puzzled me until I suddenly realised they had been burned and they were holding their arms out to prevent the painful friction of raw surfaces rubbing together. An old woman lay near me with an expression of suffering on her face; but she made no sound. Indeed, one thing was common to everyone I saw – complete silence.'

From Michihiko Hachiya, 'Hiroshima Diary'. Hachiya was a doctor in a hospital in Hiroshima in 1945.

Source D

Hiroshima after the bomb was dropped.

Questions

Section A

1 Can the Japanese have believed they could still win the war after the defeat of Germany?

2 Explain what you think Source A shows and how it would work.

3 What impression do you think the Americans can have had about Japanese determination to fight on?

4 What do you think caused the writer of Source C to lose his clothes?

5 What do you think the writer of Source B saw which upset her so much.

6 Describe the effect of dropping an atomic bomb.

Section B

7 Do you think the authors of Sources B and C agreed with Truman that he was right to drop the bomb?

8 Do you think an American soldier would agree with Truman that he was right to drop the bomb?

9 Do you think a British soldier would agree with Truman that he was right to drop the bomb?

10 Do you think someone who had lived in London through the Blitz would agree with Truman that he was right to drop the bomb?

31

Events 1945–86: The Super-powers

A

Before the Second World War, Western Europe had seemed to dominate world affairs; ever since 1945, the dominant countries have been Russia and the United States. Their wartime alliance soon broke down and although disagreements did not lead to another war, relations between the Western powers (led by the United States) and the East European states (led by Russia) were so hostile that they are referred to as the 'Cold War'. Although there have been times when the super-powers have reached agreements and been on friendlier terms, some people argue that the Cold War continues today.

B

The main reason for the Cold War and super-power hostility is the difference in political ideas (ideologies) between the Russians and the Americans. The Russians believe in **Communism** and that the state government should own all large businesses and factories so that no individual's wealth or interests can dominate the interests of the country as a whole. Communist states are 'one-party states' in which only one political party, the Communist party, is allowed. The Americans believe in **Capitalism** where individuals can own businesses and factories and are allowed to build up private wealth. The interests of different groups are represented by different political parties within a democratic system of government. Since the beginning of the Cold War both super-powers have been keen to see their own political systems used in other countries. This has led to conflicts and crises.

C

Three times the Russians have had to deal with unrest in East European countries which tried to free themselves from the soviet system – Hungary in 1956, Czechoslovakia in 1968, and Poland in 1982. The East European states led by Russia formed the Warsaw Pact in 1955 to counter NATO in the West, and their alliance depends on East European countries staying loyal to the soviet system (see Unit 35).

Communism has spread to other countries. Chinese communists, led by Mao Zedong, came to power in 1949 and their victory soon led to other communist victories in South East Asia. In a way similar to Russian interventions in Eastern Europe, the Americans have been involved in wars against the Communists in Korea 1950–53 and in Vietnam and Cambodia 1965–73. The clash of ideologies produced its most serious crisis in 1962 when there was real danger of a third world war. The Russians had supported Fidel Castro's seizure of power in Cuba in 1959 and in return had been

D

allowed to site missiles in Cuba. The United States blockaded Cuba and demanded that the Russians withdraw their missiles. The Russians agreed and this avoided another world war.

The super-powers have competed for world leadership in a variety of ways. In the space race, the Russians were the first to put a manned spacecraft into orbit; the USA landed men on the moon in 1969. The Russians were the first to establish an earth-orbiting space station; the USA was the first to develop a reuseable spacecraft – the space shuttle.

They have also competed in an arms race. The USA was the first country to develop an atomic bomb, in 1945, and the Russians exploded their atom bomb in 1949. In November 1952 the USA developed a hydrogen (thermo-nuclear) bomb, while the Russians successfully tested their first nuclear bomb in August 1953. By the early 1970s, both sides had enough nuclear weapons to blow up the world many times over.

In the Third World, the Americans have prevented most attempts to create communist governments in South America (the USA's 'back yard') and in 1973 helped to bring down a communist government elected to power in Chile. In 1984, the USA invaded the Caribbean island of Grenada when it was thought the government might turn it into a Marxist state. The Russians too have supported their allies throughout the world. One of the first was Egypt led by President Nasser in the 1950s and 1960s. Russia supported Egypt in its wars with Israel in 1967 and 1973. Similarly, Russia joined with its ally Cuba to support a Marxist takeover in Angola (1975), and invaded Afghanistan (1979).

From time to time, attempts have been made to ease the tension between the super-powers. After the Cuban Missile crisis in 1962 and the emergence of China as a nuclear power in 1964, the USA and Russia agreed to hold Strategic Arms Limitation Talks (SALT). In 1968 the five nuclear powers, USA, Russia, Great Britain, France and China, signed a Nuclear Non-Proliferation Treaty which it was hoped would stop the spread of nuclear weapons in the 1970s. The USA began a policy of **détente** to improve relations further. The Americans pulled out of the war in Vietnam in 1973 and, with the oil crisis in the West, the USA was happy to agree the SALT Treaty of 1978 which led to further limits on the spread of nuclear weapons. The movement towards arms control has led to talks at Geneva since 1984 and the summit between President Reagan and Premier Gorbachev in 1986.

E

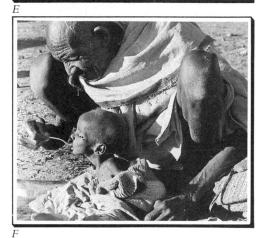

F

Questions

1 Draw a time-line showing the years 1945 to the present day. Mark on it the events referred to in the text.

2 Where on your time-line do you think each of the photographs on these pages should go?

3 Choose two pairs of photographs from the six and explain how each pair can be used to show the history of the last 40 years.

32

The United Nations

Plans for an international organisation to replace the League of Nations began soon after the Second World War broke out. In August 1941 President Roosevelt (USA) and Prime Minister Winston Churchill (GB) agreed the Atlantic Charter. In January 1942, twenty-six other friendly countries accepted the Charter and called themselves the United Nations (UN). They agreed to the principles of self determination and territorial integrity. The UN also hoped to establish political, social and economic freedom throughout the world after the war.

During the war and immediately after, various United Nations agencies were created to deal with special problems. These were:

1 **UNRRA** (United Nations Relief and Rehabilitation Administration – 1943) to provide food, medicine, equipment and clothing in countries freed from the Nazis.
2 **UNICEF** (United Nations International Childrens' Emergency Fund – 1946) to help refugee children.
3 **UNESCO** (United Nations Educational, Scientific and Cultural Organisation). This was begun in 1944 as the United Nations Organisation for Educational and Cultural Reconstruction.

Similarly, but separately, the **International Monetary Fund** (IMF) and the **World Bank** were created in 1944 to help developing countries and ensure that the world could cope with currency crises in the future.

The United Nations Organisation. ▶

Source A

A cartoon by Low, June 1945.

Source B

General Assembly
– sets the policies of the UN

Security Council
– responsible for maintaining peace and world security

Economic and Social Council – co-ordinates the economic and social work of the Council. Some of the agencies of the Council include:
- UNESCO • WHO
- UNICEF • FAO

Trusteeship Council
– promotes self-government in non-independent countries

Secretariat
– services the organisations of the UN and administers the programmes and policies laid down by them

International Court of Justice
– sits in The Hague, the Netherlands

In August 1944 the USA, Russia, Britain, China and Commonwealth countries sent representatives to a conference at Dumbarton Oaks, near Washington, to draw up plans for a United Nations Organisation (UNO). Between April and June 1945 another conference at San Francisco completed the arrangements. They agreed the United Nations Charter which includes the following important points:

1 The UNO is not allowed to interfere in the internal affairs of any of its members.
2 The UNO seeks co-operation on economic, cultural and humanitarian issues and human rights.
3 The UNO aims to promote peace and has the power to invite members to join together in the pursuit of peace. This includes the power to provide peace-keeping forces to settle disputes in war-torn countries.

The UNO is organised so that every country has one vote in the **General Assembly**, but real power lies in the **Security Council**. The Security Council has five permanent members (USA, Russia, Britain, France and China) and ten elected members. If one of the permanent members refuses to vote on an issue then no action can be taken by the UNO (this is called using a **veto**).

The UNO has its headquarters in New York and its permanent staff is headed by a **Secretary General**. At the present time a Peruvian, Javier Perez de Cuellar, elected in 1982, is the Secretary General. The work of the UNO has grown over the years and new agencies like the **World Health Organisation** (WHO), the **International Atomic Energy Association** (IAEA) and the **Food and Agriculture Organisation** (FAO) have been created.

The UNO has wide powers. It has called on its members to impose economic sanctions against countries whose policies offend the rest of the world, for example Rhodesia (Zimbabwe), and has sent forces to settle disputes, for example in the Congo (Zaire), and to keep the peace and maintain truces, for example in Lebanon.

Questions

Section A

1 In your own words, explain how the United Nations Organisation works.

2 Which of the UN agencies would you expect to be involved with the following recent events:

 a Famine in Ethiopia?
 b The Chernobyl nuclear plant explosion?

3 If the General Assembly (Source B) at the UNO has more members than the Security Council, why is the Security Council more powerful?

Section B

4 Study the cartoon (Source A). How do you think the cartoonist felt about the working of the United Nations Organisation?

5 The League of Nations, set up after the First World War, failed to preserve world peace. Are you surprised that countries were so keen in 1945 to set up another organisation to do the same job? Explain your answer.

6 Why do you think

 a the veto was written into the UNO Charter?
 b defeated countries were encouraged to join?

33

The Cold War (i): Origins and the Iron Curtain

In March 1946, Winston Churchill, visiting the USA, made a speech at Fulton, Missouri (Source A). This speech was certainly not the language of one allied leader describing another ally's action. It shows that within one year of the defeat of Germany the wartime alliance between the USA, Russia and Britain had broken down. Why did this happen? Just a year earlier in Russia, at Yalta, Roosevelt, Churchill and Stalin had reached agreement on several matters (Source B).

After Yalta the situation changed. President Roosevelt died in April – less than a month before Germany surrendered on 7 May 1945. The Russian Red Army had reached deep into Germany and by the time the Allies met again at Potsdam in July 1945, a new American President, Harry Truman, had replaced Roosevelt. As the Potsdam meeting opened, Churchill was replaced by Labour leader, Clement Attlee.

Truman was convinced that the Russians were not going to hold free elections in Poland and other eastern European countries. Stalin had already invited non-communist Polish leaders to Moscow where they had been arrested. In June a Provisional Government was set up in Poland in which the key posts were given to Polish Communists. Truman thought that he could take a tough line with the Russians because on 17 July, the day the conference began in Potsdam, the United States successfully exploded the first ever atomic bomb. However, Stalin would not give way, and all that was agreed at Potsdam were arrangements concerning Germany (Source C).

Source A

'From Stettin in the Baltic to Trieste in the Adriatic, an iron curtain has descended…. Behind that line lie all the capitals of the states of central and eastern Europe – all are subject in one form or another not only to Soviet influence but to a very high and increasing measure of control from Moscow.'

Winston Churchill speaking at Fulton, Missouri, 1946.

Source B

The Yalta accords

1 Germany to be disarmed, demilitarised and divided into four zones of occupation by Britain, the USA, France and Russia.
2 Germany to pay reparations of which half to go to Russia.
3 Germany to be **denazified** (Nazism stamped out) and the Nazi leaders put on trial.
4 Countries once occupied by Germany to be free to elect their own governments.
5 Poland to give back land taken from Russia in 1921. In return, Poland to be given German territory to its west.
6 The allies to sign a treaty of friendship and alliance with China, and Russia to join the war against Japan after the defeat of Germany.
7 A United Nations Organisation to be created.

Source C

The Potsdam agreement

1 German-speaking people in Poland, Czechoslovakia and Hungary to be transferred to Germany.
2 Germany to be administered by a control council made up of the four military commanders of the occupied zones.
3 Nazi leaders to be put on trial at Nuremberg and SS men hunted down.
4 Each power to take what war reparations it wanted from its own zone and Russia also to be allowed to remove a quarter of the industrial equipment in the British and American zones.

American fears of Russia in 1946	Russian fears of the USA in 1946
1 The Russians' aim to spread Communism. 2 Russian military expansion into Eastern Europe. 3 Russian actions in Germany.	1 American support for the capitalist system throughout the world. 2 Fear of attack from the West and need for friendly governments bordering Russia. 3 Fear of the US atomic bomb.

The two great powers, Russia and the USA, were convinced that the other wanted to destroy its way of life. It is easy to see why the Americans and the Russians distrusted each other by 1946.

Winston Churchill's 'iron curtain' speech at Fulton is sometimes referred to as the announcement of the **Cold War** (so-called because there was no actual fighting between the Americans and Russians, only a war of words and deep suspicion and hostility). However, after 1946 there were many occasions when the world feared that the Cold War would become a real war.

Europe divided by the Iron Curtain.

Questions

Section A

1 Draw the map, marking on the Iron Curtain. List those countries that were 'behind' the Iron Curtain.

2 Study Source A. The Iron Curtain was not a real wall of iron. It later became a barbed wire border. What do you think Churchill wanted to suggest by using the words 'iron curtain'?

3 Which one of the seven points agreed at Yalta caused most disagreement at Potsdam? Why do you think the disagreement happened (Sources B and C)?

4 Explain in your own words what is meant by 'the Cold War'.

Section B

5 Make a list of the important events which occurred between the meetings at Yalta and Potsdam.

6 Write a paragraph which explains how the Second World War ended and the Cold War began.

7 What was the key event in the relationship between Russia and the United States – when they stopped being allies and started being enemies? Give reasons to explain your choice.

34

The Cold War (ii): The Division of Germany

In March 1947 President Truman announced the **Truman Doctrine**. The Americans had decided to help rebuild countries in Western Europe to counter the spread of Communism. In April 1947, General Marshall was sent to Europe to investigate the situation in the countries struggling to recover from the effects of war, and in June 1947 he announced the **Marshall Plan**. This gave aid to countries which asked for it. General Marshall said: 'Any country that is willing to assist in the task of recovery will find full co-operation from the US government'. Aid was to be available to any country, including Russia, but the Russian press denounced the plan as 'a new alliance against Communism', and Stalin refused to allow any East European country to receive aid. Russia believed that governments in Eastern Europe must remain friendly to it. The Truman Doctrine and the Marshall Plan were examples of an American policy known as **containment**. The USA had decided to 'contain' Communism behind the Iron Curtain. The first test of the policy came in 1948 in Germany.

At Yalta it had been agreed to divide Germany into zones of occupation. The Potsdam agreement had added that Germany would be administered jointly by a Control Council, and have to pay reparation demands, and that Germans would be transferred from Eastern Europe to Germany. However, the effects of these measures had been to weaken Germany. The country's overall production had fallen to only 27 per cent of what it had been before the war, and more than one person in five was starving.

In January 1948 the Americans and British announced that they were combining their occupation zones into one unit called **Bizonia**. On 25 February the Communists took control of the government in Czechoslovakia. There was now a clear division between Russia and the USA. In March, the Russians walked out of a Control Council meeting because the USA, Britain and France would not reveal their plans for the future of their zones. Events moved quickly after this meeting. Russia closed the road, rail and waterway links to West Berlin. The Western powers supplied their sectors by a massive airlift. This airlift might have led to war if the Russians had tried to stop it. The US B29 Bombers could carry atomic bombs and the Russians were not to know if any did. The chance that a real war might start may have deterred the Russians. However, the statements of both sides show very clearly that the Cold War had truly begun.

From the speech in which President Truman announced the Truman Doctrine

'At the present moment in history nearly every nation must choose between alternate ways of life. The choice is too often not a free one. One way of life is based upon the will of the majority and is distinguished by free institutions.... The second way of life is based upon the will of the minority, forcibly imposed on the majority. [It] relies upon terror and oppression, a controlled press, fixed elections and the suppression of personal freedom.'

Source B

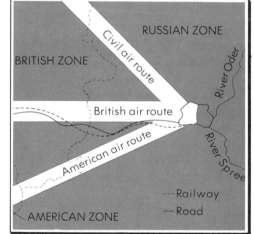

Routes into Berlin.

Events in Germany 1948 – 9

US/British actions

1 January 1948 – Britain and the USA create **Bizonia** out of their parts of Germany. It receives a small amount of Marshall aid.
2 18 June 1948 – Western zones introduce a new currency (the *Deutschmark*) to replace the old, almost worthless currency (*Reichsmark*).
3 June 1948 – 12 May 1949, the Americans and British airlift goods and supplies into Berlin in B29 Bombers.
4 12 May 1949 – the Federal Republic of Germany is created with its capital, Bonn.

Source C

Berliners watch the Allied planes.

Source D

'The Soviet authorities were ready to provide food and fuel for the population of the whole of Berlin, but the Western powers deprived the inhabitants of help from Eastern Germany. The USA organised a so-called 'airlift' [which] served the purposes of propaganda.'

Adapted from a Russian news statement.

Russian actions

1 March 1948 – Russian walk-out from Control Council meeting (Britain, France and USA refuse to reveal future plans for their zone).

2 19 June 1948 – Russians introduce a new currency of their own.

3 24 June 1948 – Russians close roads, rail, and waterway links with West Berlin.

4 7 October 1949 – Russians refuse to allow any political parties except the Communist party in their zone, and create the German Democratic Republic.

Source E

'When we refused to be forced out of the city of Berlin, we demonstrated to the people of Europe that with their co-operation we would act…. when their freedom was threatened.'

President Truman.

Questions

Section A

1 What was the Truman Doctrine (Source A) and why did it come to be American policy from 1947?

2 Explain what President Truman meant when he said 'The Truman Doctrine and the Marshall Plan were always two halves of the same walnut'.

3 Why would Russia claim that Marshall Aid was aimed at 'uniting countries on an anti-Soviet basis'?

4 Explain 'containment' in your own words.

5 Do you think Source C is from a Russian or an American magazine?

Section B

6 Copy and complete the chart which follows

American/British action	Russian response
a Announcement of Truman Doctrine and Marshall Aid.	?
b Extension of Marshall Aid to Bizonia.	?
c Introduction of currency reforms in Western Zone.	?
d Creation of the Federal Republic.	?

Russian action	American/British response
a Support of takeover of East European governments by Communist parties.	?
b Russian walk-out from Control Council.	?
c Russian blockade of Berlin.	?
d May 1949 Russians lift blockade.	?

7 Study the chart you have completed. How does it show the difficulties of explaining the causes of the division of Germany?

8 Study Sources D and E. Both the Americans and the Russians claim the Berlin crisis was caused by the other. Is it possible to place all the blame on one side? Explain your answer.

35

The Cold War (iii): Confrontation in Europe

Events in Germany had shown that the different ideologies of the USA and Russia could lead to conflict. Between 1949 and 1955 both countries made defensive alliances as the Cold War intensified. Why was there so much mistrust?

The situation through American eyes

The 'iron curtain' speech by Winston Churchill and the Truman Doctrine both show that the West believed Russia was prepared to spread Communism by force. Long before the Second World War western governments had feared the spread of communist revolution and were well aware of the aims of Communism laid down in Karl Marx's *Communist Manifesto*, first published in 1848: 'Let the ruling classes tremble at communist revolution. The proletarians have nothing to lose but their chains. They have a world to win. Working men of all countries unite'.

While the Nazis had been a common enemy the West had cooperated with Russia, but by the time of the Potsdam conference things had begun to change. American Secretary of State J.F. Byrnes summed up the American position: 'Only by refusing to bow to Soviet domination could we establish sound relations for the future'. The successful use of the atomic bomb changed American attitudes to Russia. President Truman became far more confident and aggressive. Byrnes advised Truman that 'the bomb might well put us in a position to dictate our own terms'.

The actions of President Truman can be seen against this background, but the Berlin blockade showed that the Russians still had vast military power which they could use. Individually, the western countries were not powerful enough to resist Russia and so, in April 1949, twelve states signed the North Atlantic Treaty, later to be joined by the Federal Republic of Germany, Greece and Turkey.

The situation through Russian eyes

Russia had paid a terrible price for victory in the Second World War. More than 20,000,000 of its people were killed. Russians were determined to be safe against future attack and to spread Communism to neighbouring countries to ensure friendly governments in the states closest to them.

When the Americans dropped the atomic bomb on

Source A

'The parties to this Treaty reaffirm their faith in the purposes and principles of the Charter of the United Nations and their desire to live in peace with all peoples and all governments. They are determined to safeguard the freedom, common heritage and civilization of their peoples, founded on the principles of democracy, individual liberty and the rule of law. They seek to promote stability and well-being in the North Atlantic area. They are resolved to unite their efforts for collective defence and for the preservation of peace and security.

The parties agree that an armed attack against one or more of them in Europe or North America should be considered an attack against them all.'

The North Atlantic Treaty.

Source B

An extract from the Warsaw Pact Treaty

'In accordance with the pact of friendship, co-operation and mutual assistance between the People's Republic of Albania … the Hungarian People's Republic … the Union of Soviet Socialist Republics and the Czechoslovak Republic, the signatory states have decided to set up a unified command of armed forces … taking into consideration at the same time the situation which has arisen in Europe … the formation of a new military alignment in the form of the West European Union with the participation of Western Germany, which is being remilitarised, and her inclusion in the North Atlantic bloc, which increases the danger of a new war….'

Hiroshima on 6 August 1945 the Russians saw that they could be attacked across the North Pole by American bombers. They decided to develop their own atomic weapons to counter the Americans and, after the creation of NATO, to build up their own system of alliances.

By the end of July 1949 the Russians had exploded their own atomic bomb and had helped the Communists to power in China with the creation of the People's Republic of China in October 1949. Early in 1950 the People's Republic signed a thirty-year treaty of alliance with Russia.

In Eastern Europe the Russians began to develop answers to the growing economic and military unity in the West. In January 1949 Russia headed a group of six other European States to form COMECON, the Russian answer to Marshall Aid and the OEEC (Organisation for European Economic Co-operation) which had been formed in 1948.

In May 1955 the Russians joined with other East European governments to form the Warsaw Pact as an answer to NATO.

Source C

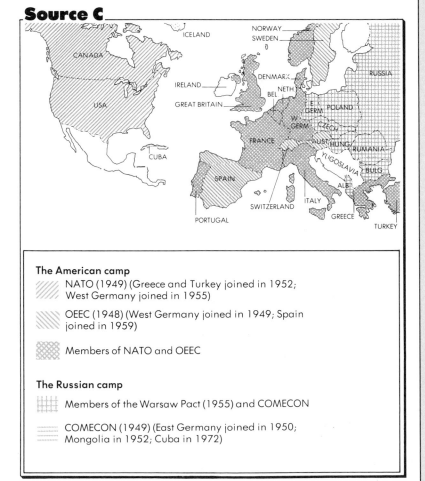

The American camp

NATO (1949) (Greece and Turkey joined in 1952; West Germany joined in 1955)

OEEC (1948) (West Germany joined in 1949; Spain joined in 1959)

Members of NATO and OEEC

The Russian camp

Members of the Warsaw Pact (1955) and COMECON

COMECON (1949) (East Germany joined in 1950; Mongolia in 1952; Cuba in 1972)

The US and Russian camps.

Questions

Section A

1 In class discuss the word **ideology**. What is meant when it is said that the differences between the USA and Russia are a result of the different ideologies of Capitalism and Communism?

2 Study Source C.
  a Make a table showing the countries in the Warsaw Pact and in NATO.
  b Which European countries can you think of which are non-aligned (not on one side or the other)?

Section B

3 a Study Sources A and B. In what ways do NATO and the Warsaw Pact seem to have the same aims?
  b If the aims are similar, why were the alliances considered necessary?

4 The Americans agreed to the NATO alliance which aimed to 'safeguard freedom [of all peoples]...founded on the principles of *democracy*'. The Russians created the German *Democratic* Republic. Why did the Americans then fear the Russians?

5 The Russians claimed that NATO was an anti-soviet alliance. Which of the following statements do you think might explain the Russian attitude? Give reasons for your answer.
  a The Americans wanted to encircle Russia with hostile states so that they might eventually destroy Communism.
  b The Americans wanted to extend Capitalism to all the countries of the world.
  c The Americans wanted bases for their aeroplanes to threaten Russia with atomic bombs.

71

36

The Korean War

After 1949 the Chinese, like the Russians, were committed to spreading Communism to other countries.

During the Second World War, the Japanese had occupied most of South East Asia and Indo-China. In 1945 Japanese forces in the North had surrendered to the Russians, while in the South they had surrendered to the Americans. The result of this, in Korea, was that two separate governments were created north and south of the 38th parallel. A communist government in the North was led by Kim Il Sung, and a non-communist government in the South was led by President Syngman Rhee.

On 25 June 1950 North Korean forces, armed with Russian weapons, invaded South Korea and, within three days, captured the capital, Seoul. The Americans sent help to the South Koreans. The Americans also managed to get the support of the United Nations as the Russians had walked out a few months earlier because Communist China was not allowed to join. The UN agreed 'to furnish such assistance to the Republic of Korea as may be necessary to repel the armed attack and to restore peace and security in the area'.

As a result other countries, including Britain, sent troops to join the Americans and to aid South Korea. At first the UN forces were pinned down in a narrow area in the South around Pusan, but on 15 September they attacked the communist troops on land and from the sea near Inchon. There was fierce fighting around Seoul with many civilian casualties, but by October the communist forces were retreating across the 38th parallel.

On 7 October the Americans began to pursue the Communists northwards and on 10 October the Chinese announced that if the pursuit continued they would be forced to enter the war against the UN forces. By 24 October the UN troops were pressing on towards the Yalu river (the border with China). Within a fortnight the Chinese had entered the war and, using the tactic of the 'human flood', had driven the Americans back. By mid January, the American general, MacArthur, had suffered the humiliation of being forced to retreat across the 38th parallel.

MacArthur began to fight back and, by February 1951, had pushed the Communists back across the 38th parallel. President Truman, relieved that **containment** seemed possible, began to plan a negotiated cease-fire but MacArthur attacked the Chinese, demanding their surrender. He wanted to destroy Communism, and reinstate Chiang Kai Shek as leader of China, and had even talked about the use of nuclear weapons. Truman was not prepared to run the risk of a third

Source A

'It seems strangely difficult for some to realise that here in Asia is where the Communist conspirators have elected to make their play for global conquest ... that here we fight Europe's war with arms while the diplomats there still fight it with words, that if we lose the war to Communism in Asia the fall of Europe is inevitable. There is no substitute for victory.'

General MacArthur, 1950.

Source B

North and South Korea.

Source C

'They are peculiarly vulnerable to the process of blockade, and the process of internal disruption by bombing. The minute you apply these factors it is difficult for them to maintain an army on the march.

...the best way to stop any surprise attack by the Soviet Union is to impress on him that the power we possess is sufficient, if he goes to war, to overpower him.'

General MacArthur on his return to the USA, April 1951.

world war. He believed that if Communist China was threatened the Russians might join in the war, and so, on 11 April 1951, MacArthur was sacked.

The chances of a quick end to the war were unlikely. Both sides had 'dug in' around the 38th parallel, and neither had air supremacy. MacArthur had believed he could ignore the orders of his commander-in-chief but had paid the price for exceeding his authority.

The Truman–MacArthur controversy: who was right?

President Truman told General MacArthur that American involvement in Korea had the following aims:

- To demonstrate to the free world that the USA was prepared to meet the communist threat with force.
- To humiliate Communist China in the eyes of its neighbours.
- To provide time to organise resistance to Communism in Asia.
- To show the South Koreans that the USA was loyal to its allies.
- To encourage resistance to Communism throughout the world.
- To prove that the United Nations Organisation could be effective.

The dismissal of MacArthur stunned the American people. The general was very popular and on his return he claimed that the Chinese could have been beaten and that the Russians would have been too scared to intervene. However, many American officials disagreed with MacArthur – the American Secretary of State, Dean Acheson, for one. In the end a truce was agreed between the North and South; a final peace treaty had to wait until after President Truman had retired from office.

Source D

'We know of Soviet influence in North Korea. We know that there is a treaty between the Soviets and the Chinese Communists. It is difficult to see how the Soviet Union could ignore a direct attack upon the Chinese mainland.'

Dean Acheson.

Questions

Section A

1 Draw a time-line to show the events of the Korean War.

2 Copy the map of Korea and use different coloured arrows and a key to show:
   a The initial North Korean invasion.
   b The American break out from Pusan and landing at Inchon.
   c The American and UN pursuit of the retreating North Koreans.
   d The Chinese invasion and march south.
   e The eventual positions of both sides.

3 Which of the United States' aims would you say **were** achieved during the Korean War?

4 Which of the United States' aims would you say **were not** achieved during the Korean War?

Section B

5 Study Source A.
   a Which words or phrases does MacArthur use which are intended to turn the reader against the Communists?
   b Explain how MacArthur suggests that a 'hot' war in the Far East reflects the 'Cold War' between the super-powers.

6 Sources C and D contradict each other about the chances of a successful American attack on China. Which of the following statements best explains the contradiction? Give reasons for your answer.

   a General MacArthur was biased. He wanted to prove himself and he believed in a crusade against Communism.
   b General MacArthur did not have a 'global view'. He only knew about the situation in the Far East.
   c Dean Acheson and the American administration were frightened to take risks. MacArthur was not afraid to risk a third world war.

7 How would a historian check the reliability of Acheson's and MacArthur's statements?

37

Russia and Eastern Europe (i): Hungary 1956

The Warsaw Pact had bound Eastern European countries into an alliance with Russia. Many of the people in these states resented the Russian-style Communism which was forced on them by their governments. Those who spoke against their governments were often arrested without trial, as had happened under Joseph Stalin in Russia until his death in March 1953.

In February 1956 the Soviet leader, Nikita Krushchev, denounced Stalinism in a speech to the Russian Communist party. Many people in Eastern Europe took this as a sign that they also could protest against the Communist governments under which they lived. In July a revolt against low standards of living and low wages broke out in Poland. Although the Polish revolt was quickly crushed, unrest spread to Hungary and to the capital Budapest. Students, trade unionists and officers in the army united against the hated communist leader, Matyas Rakosi.

Street fighting in Budapest lasted for five days and forced the withdrawal of the Russian troops on 28 October (Source B). However, by 4 November, the Russians were back and Hungarian radio stations broadcast desperate messages for help from the West (Source D).

The Hungarians believed that the Americans and the Western European governments would help them because throughout the early years of the Cold War, western radio stations had broadcast messages encouraging East European peoples to stand up for their freedom. However, no western help ever came to the Hungarians, despite their demands for an end to one-party government and for free elections. By the middle of November the revolt was over. More than 30,000 Hungarians had been killed and 200,000 fled abroad. The prime minister, Imre Nagy, who had been forced to give in to the demands of the rebels, was imprisoned and later shot.

Source A

'The first evening I saw a man with a rifle appear. He took up position in one of the drives and taking careful aim, began shooting out the street lamps. Quite soon after there were flashes of gunfire and sounds of battle and we saw wrecked and burning buildings in the streets of Budapest.'

Source B

'The first to see the unfamiliar face of freedom were the young rebels. Their weapons at the ready, their faces filthy with the grime of battle, their clothes often blood-caked, they stood along the streets, happily jeering the departing Soviet tanks as they rumbled sullenly by.

Only a few hours before, desperate battles had been fought at the Maria Theresa barracks, at the Communist party headquarters, and at the steel mills at Cespel island. With their heavy 76 mm guns, the soviet tanks had attempted to blast the rebels out of their hiding places, but the "incredible youngsters" had evolved their own technique for dealing with the mighty 26-ton tanks. First they would fire on the tanks from the upper-storey windows, then as the big T-34s rumbled up, their great guns elevated, a small boy would leap out of a doorway, fling a pail of gasoline over the tank's engine compartment and leap back to the shelter.'

From 'Five Days of Freedom', in 'Time Magazine', 12 November 1956.

Source C

A statue of Stalin toppled in Budapest City Park and dragged through the streets.

Eye witness account by a Russian tourist, 23 October 1956.

Source D

A Russian tank controls a Budapest street, November 1956.

Source E

'Civilised people of the world! Our ship is sinking. Light is fading. The shadows grow darker over the soil of Hungary. Extend us your aid.'

Budapest Radio broadcast.

Questions

Section A

1 Copy the following statements matching each head with its correct tail.

Heads	Tails
a The Warsaw Pact had bound Eastern European countries into an alliance with the Soviet Union.	Hungarian students, army officers and trade unionists wanted to overthrow the Communist leader Matyas Rakosi.
b In 1956 a revolt broke out in Budapest.	Because of radio broadcasts the Hungarians expected help from the Americans and Western European governments.
c For many years western radio stations had broadcast messages encouraging East Europeans to stand up for their freedom.	Imre Nagy was imprisoned and shot because he gave in to the demands of the rebels.
d The Hungarians wanted an end to one-party government, and free elections.	Many people distrusted this system of Russian-style Communism.

2 What part did the following people or groups play in the Hungarian revolution?

    a Matyas Rakosi   **b** Students   **c** Russian tanks
    d Imre Nagy   **e** Nikita Krushchev

Section B

3 Complete the chain of causation which led to the outbreak of the Hungarian revolution.

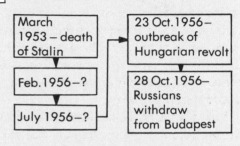

4 **a** Which of the sources is least helpful in explaining why the revolt took place? Explain your choice.
  b Which source is most helpful in explaining why the revolt took place? Explain your choice.

5 **a** Were the following causes of the Hungarian revolution? Give reasons for your answer in **each** case.
   i Unhappiness about living standards and working conditions.
   ii Discontent with communist government.
   iii 'Freedom' broadcasts from western radio stations.
   iv The actions of Nikita Krushchev.
   v Military help from the Americans.
  b Which of the above list do you think was the **most** important cause of the Hungarian revolution? Explain your answer.

75

38

The Cold War (iv): The Berlin Wall

Berlin, a city deep inside East Germany, had been divided into communist and non–communist zones since 1945. After the great tension at the time of the Berlin Airlift life in the city had become a little easier. Thousands of Berliners crossed the Russian and Allied sectors of the city to work or to visit family. However, on 13 August 1961 this changed. In the morning the East German border guards would not let anybody cross and a barbed-wire fence was built dividing the city into two. By the end of August this was replaced by a permanent wall.

The Berlin Wall was the 'bricks and concrete manifestation of the Cold War', claimed one western newspaper. The wall made the division of Europe into a reality. Until it was built more than two million refugees crossed from East to West. This was very embarrassing to Russia which was proclaiming the wonderful life that people would enjoy in soviet-style East European states. Watch-towers and machine-gun posts were soon added to the wall. The East German authorities claimed it was to keep spies out, but anyone attempting to escape across the wall was likely to be shot. Forty-one people were killed trying to cross in the twelve months after August 1961.

In 1962, US President Kennedy visited Western Europe and went to Berlin. He had been accused of being 'soft on

Source A

The Berlin wall separates East Berlin from West Berlin. In East Berlin, beyond the wall, stands the Brandenburg Gate.

Source B

From Kennedy's speech in Berlin

'All free men, wherever they may be, are citizens of Berlin and thus I take pride in saying "*Ich bin ein Berliner*".'

Communism' because he had not ordered his troops to tear down the wall. He made a rousing speech which attacked the soviet system, but made no real promises to reopen the border.

In August 1986 demonstrations took place to mark the twenty-fifth anniversary of the building of the Berlin Wall. Many western leaders continue to condemn the wall as a symbol of Russian oppression and a barrier to freedom. They mourned the many people who had died trying to escape over the wall, but the division of Germany and Europe is now accepted as permanent.

Source C

American and Russian tanks face each other at the Friedrichstrasse checkpoint.

Source D

East Germans complain about grave provocation by West

Protesters launch assault on Berlin wall

Several hundred young conservatives belonging to Chancellor Helmut Kohl's Christian Democratic Party were involved in a tense encounter with East German border guards at the weekend in protests against the Berlin wall, built 25 years ago this week.

West Berlin police said that about 200 young people, most from West Germany, crossed the demarcation line, hurled fireworks and stones, and tore down an East German flag.

British military police detained a man, aged 30, who started a fire on the wall near the Reichstag building.

From the 'Guardian', Monday 11 August 1986.

Questions

Section A

1 a Why did the Russian/East German authorities say that they had built the Berlin Wall?
  b What other reasons might they have had?

2 a What signs of tension between the powers can be seen in Source B?
  b Do you think Source C was taken before or after the Berlin Wall was built? Give reasons for your answer.

3 Why do you think the western powers did not tear down the Berlin Wall in 1961?

Section B

4 Study Sources A and C. In 1958 Nikita Kruschev announced: 'We shall never change our mind about the German problem'. How would you explain this Russian attitude and the decision to make the division of Germany permanent?

5 What do you think President Kennedy meant when he said, 'Ich bin ein Berliner [I am a Berliner]'? How do you think each of the following would have reacted to this statement?

  a An American
  b A Russian
  c A West German

6 Study Source D. The Berlin Wall had existed for twenty-five years. Why did West Germans still want to protest against it?

39

The Cold War (v): The Cuban Missile Crisis

In 1959 President Batista of Cuba was overthrown by the revolutionary army of the Marxist Fidel Castro. In 1961 the American CIA supported an invasion of Cuba by Cuban exiles to try to overthrow Castro and return Batista to power. The invasion took place at the Bay of Pigs but was easily beaten off.

The American action in supporting the invasion played into the hands of Castro who could now claim that he needed to draw closer to Russia because of American hostility. The Russians knew that the USA had a fairly inexperienced president, whereas the Russian leader, Nikita Krushchev, had been in power some years. Russia was concerned that it was surrounded by American nuclear bases and decided that it too should have missile bases close to the USA. Once the Russians had made their decision to send missiles to Cuba, a chain of events followed which brought the world to the brink of nuclear war. The crisis began on 1 September and did not end until 28 October. After the crisis in 1963 both sides agreed to set up a hot-line (direct telephone link) between Moscow and Washington to give leaders instant communication with each other.

Source A

'Your rockets are situated in Britain, situated in Italy, and are aimed against us. Your rockets are situated in Turkey. You are worried by Cuba. You say that it worries you because it is a distance of ninety miles by sea from the coast of America, but Turkey is next to us. I therefore make this proposal: we agree to remove from Cuba those means which you regard as offensive means; we agree to carry this out and make a pledge in the United Nations. Your representatives will make a declaration to the effect that the United States, on its part, considering the uneasiness and anxiety of the Soviet State, will remove its similar means from Turkey...'

Letter from Krushchev to Kennedy.

Source B

'I have received your message of 27th October.... So as to eliminate as rapidly as possible the conflict which is endangering peace... the Soviet Government, in addition to the earlier instructions to cease further work on the weapon-construction sites, has given a new order to dismantle those arms which you have described as offensive, to crate them, and return them to the Soviet Union....'

Letter from Krushchev to Kennedy.

An outline of events during the Cuban crisis

17 April 1961 Bay of Pigs invasion by Cubans in American ships. Defeated.

13 August 1961 Berlin Wall built (Cold War intensifies).

18 November 1961 Russia announces successful explosion of 58-megaton nuclear bomb.

1 September 1962 CIA learns of Russian bases in Cuba.

16 October 1962 American spy-planes (U2s) photograph missile launching sites in Cuba. American committee of National Security Council discusses response. Three alternatives were:
1 A nuclear attack on Cuba by USA.
2 An invasion.
3 A blockade of the island.

22 October 1962 USA decides on a blockade to stop Russian ships carrying missiles.

25 October 1962 American navy intercepts Russian ships.

26 October 1962 Krushchev writes to Kennedy asking for promise that USA will not attack Cuba.

27 October 1962 Krushchev sends a second letter and offers to remove Cuban bases if American nuclear bases in Turkey are removed. Kennedy replies to Krushchev's first letter and promises USA will not invade Cuba.

28 October 1962 Krushchev agrees to remove missiles.

Source D

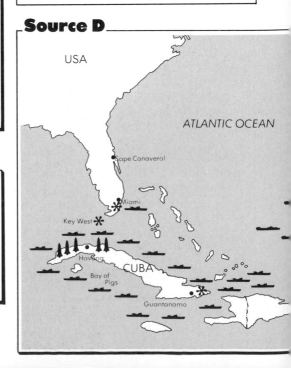

Source C

'If assurances were given that the President of the United States would not participate in an attack on Cuba and the blockade (were) lifted, then the removal or the destruction of the missile sites in Cuba would be an entirely different question. We and you ought not to pull on the ends of a rope in which you have tied the knot of war, because the more the two of us pull, the tighter that knot will be tied. Let us not only relax the forces pulling on the ends of the rope, let us take measures to untie that knot. We are ready for this.'

Letter from Krushchev to Kennedy.

Russian ship approaching Cuba, photographed from an American aircraft

✳ US air bases

⎯ US naval blockade

⬍ Russian missile bases

⎯ Russian ships

PUERTO
RICO
✳
(USA)

Questions

Section A

1 The beginnings and endings of the following sentences have been mixed up. Match the correct heads and tails.

	Heads	Tails
a	Before 1960 Cuba had traditionally been friendly	to have a Russian missile base in Cuba.
b	Castro's revolutionary government in Cuba was not friendly towards the USA	and better communications were set up between the two countries to try and avoid such a thing happening again.
c	The Cubans secretly arranged with Russia	the world was on the edge of war.
d	This alarmed the USA because	with the United States.
e	President Kennedy (the American leader) demanded that the Russian missiles should be withdrawn,	because of the help the USA gave to the Bay of Pigs invasion.
f	Finally Russia agreed to take the missiles away,	Cuba is so close to America.

2 What do you understand by the term 'brinkmanship'? At what point do you think **a** Russia **b** the USA were guilty of brinkmanship?

3 Study the map. How difficult would it have been for the USA to:
   a attack Cuba with nuclear missiles?
   b invade Cuba?
   c blockade Cuba?
   Why do you think President Kennedy chose option **c**?

Section B

4 What date should be given to each of the Sources A, B and C? Give reasons for your answer in each case.

5 Why is it important to know these dates when judging the skill in Kennedy's response to Krushchev?

6 Which of the events before October 1962 would you say were most important in shaping:
   a Russian attitudes to the crisis?
   b American attitudes to the crisis?

7 How do you explain the decision to set up a hot-line in 1963?

40

The Arms Race

From 1945 onwards the fear that one side might become more powerful than the other led to an arms race between the USA and Russia. By 1953, both had developed hydrogen bombs. So, by 1968, had Britain, France and China.

Perhaps worried by the Cuban crisis of 1962 Russia and the USA began talks to cut down on their huge stocks of arms. The first step came in 1963 when they agreed to stop testing nuclear weapons in the atmosphere, and in 1968 a Nuclear Non-proliferation Treaty was signed to prevent the spread of nuclear weapons to other countries.

After Richard Nixon became President of the United States in 1968 he improved relations with Russia. Nixon appointed a chief adviser on foreign affairs, Henry Kissinger, who worked on a policy of co-operation and relaxation of tension known as **détente**. In 1969, Russia and the USA agreed to hold Strategic Arms Limitation Talks (SALT) and an agreement was reached in 1972 limiting certain types of weapons on both sides.

In 1979 a SALT 2 treaty was drawn up which further limited nuclear weapons not covered by SALT 1. However, this treaty was never ratified (finally agreed) by the USA because of new fears about Russia. On Christmas Day 1979, Russian troops invaded Afghanistan, and the western powers were outraged. *Détente* came to a sudden end.

In 1980, Ronald Reagan became President of the USA and was determined to increase American military spending further. The Russians deployed hundreds of new 'SS-20' medium-range missiles and NATO agreed that 450 American 'Cruise' and 'Pershing' missiles should be based in Western Europe to counter them.

In 1981, the USA announced that it had developed a 'neutron' bomb that could kill millions of people without damaging too many buildings. In 1982 President Reagan decided to develop new multi-warhead MX missiles as part of his renewal of American defence systems.

The renewed arms build-up led to massive peace protests in the West, with large demonstrations in most Western European countries. In the UK a women's peace camp was set up permanently outside the Cruise missile base at Greenham Common. Western European Governments, however, still largely voted in favour of keeping the missiles, with only the Danish parliament voting against.

In January 1984, the USA successfully destroyed a missile in flight by using a space satellite laser gun. This allowed

The development of nuclear weapons

1945 (August) USA drops atomic bombs on Hiroshima and Nagasaki

1949 (July) Russian atomic bomb exploded

1952 (October) British atomic bomb (November) US hydrogen bomb

1953 (August) Russian hydrogen bomb

1954 (January) US nuclear-powered submarine, USS *Nautilus*, launched

1957 (May) British hydrogen bomb (August) Russian intercontinental ballistic missile (ICBM) (October) Russian launching of the first spacecraft, *Sputnik 1* (December) US Atlas ICBM

1960 (February) French atomic bomb (July) US submarine *George Washington* fires Polaris missile with nuclear warhead

1963 (August) Nuclear Test Ban Treaty between USA and Russia

1964 (October) Chinese atomic bomb

1966 (September) First British nuclear submarine fitted with Polaris missiles

1967 (June) Chinese hydrogen bomb

1968 (July) Nuclear Non-proliferation Treaty between USA and Russia – within a year joined by Britain and eighty-three other countries (August) French hydrogen bomb

1974 (May) Indian atomic device exploded

Source A

The peace camp at Greenham Common.

President Reagan to announce his Strategic Defence Initiative (SDI) which became known as Star Wars. Early in 1985, Reagan invited European governments to join in SDI research with the aim of creating an 'umbrella in space' of satellite weapons which could destroy all ICBMs and put an end to mutually assured destruction (MAD). The Russians attacked the plan as a 'dangerous escalation of the arms race' but they agreed to Reagan's proposals to begin Strategic Arms Reduction Talks (START) at Geneva. President Reagan proposed the 'zero-option', by which the USA offered to scrap its plans to deploy Cruise in Europe if the USSR would dismantle its SS-20s. The Russians walked out of the Geneva talks in 1985, but after Mikhail Gorbachev became the Russian leader later that year, fear of SDI and the deployment of Cruise missiles led to renewed talks. Reagan and Gorbachev met in Geneva in 1985 and at Reykjavik (Iceland) in 1986, but the USA refused to abandon research into SDI and so the Russians refused to reach any agreement. Mr Gorbachev summed up the meeting by saying: 'This has been a failure, and failure when we were very close to a historic agreement'.

Source B

The path of an ICBM (intercontinental ballistic missile).

Strategic Defence Initiative – 'Star Wars'.

Questions

Section A

1 What important events in the history of arms control occurred in the following years?

   a 1963, b 1969, c 1972, d 1979, e 1986

2 Does Source A prove that the British people were more worried about nuclear weapons in the 1980s than at any other time since 1945?

Section B

3 a Draw a time-line showing the years 1945–87.
   b Shade in red on your time-line the following periods of international tension: the Berlin crisis, the Korean war, the Cuban Missile Crisis, the invasion of Afghanistan.
   c Mark on your time-line the key developments of weapons by Russia and the USA.
   d Mark on your time-line the important attempts to control or limit nuclear weapons.

4 Can you see any connection between the times of greatest tension between Russia and the USA and the development of new weapons?

5 Can you see any connection between the times of greatest tension between Russia and the USA and attempts to control nuclear weapons?

6 Can you see any connection between the development of new weapons and attempts to control nuclear weapons?

7 If attempts to limit the spread of nuclear weapons could be called the Peace Race, do you think historians will look back at the years covered by this unit and call them the Arms Race or the Peace Race? Give reasons for your answer.

81

41

The Space Race

'One small step for man, a giant leap for mankind.' These words were used by Neil Armstrong as he became the first human to land on the moon in 1969. President Nixon described the moon landing as the 'greatest week in the history of the world since the Creation', and it certainly seemed so to those watching the event on television around the globe. Russia had launched the first spacecraft, *Sputnik 1* in October 1957 and just over twelve years later humans were on the moon.

In these twelve years the USA and Russia competed for international prestige in space. It was not prestige, however, which was the real reason for the space race. Nuclear weapons needed delivery systems and military rockets had been developed since the use of V1 and V2 rockets by the Germans in the Second World War. The Russians had a head start – a second Sputnik was launched with the dog Laika on board – and, in trying to catch up with *Sputnik 1*, the USA had eight failures in eleven attempts before the successful launch of *Explorer 1* in January 1958.

On 12 April 1961, Yuri Gagarin became the first cosmonaut when he orbited the earth in *Vostok 1*. The North American Space Agency (NASA) at Cape Canaveral (later renamed Cape Kennedy) was unable to match the Russian achievement at first. The American rockets were light-weight and although, in 1961, they also put men into space, it was only possible to fire them into space and then return them straight to earth. It was not until 1962 that the Americans were able to orbit the earth. By 1963 six astronauts and six cosmonauts had been put into space. It seemed as if both sides were keeping score, and the Russians still had the edge with Valentina Tereshkova becoming the first woman cosmonaut.

The next stage in the race was to put spacecraft with more than one person on board into orbit. The first successful stage of the American Gemini programme saw the two-man space-crafts make a rendezvous in space. The Russians upstaged this by launching the three-man Voshkod, and performing the first space walk.

In 1969 the Russians organised a link-up between three spacecraft and seven cosmonauts. The Americans overshadowed this achievement by the successful moon landing on 20 July in the same year. After the success of the American moon programme the space race continued, but along different paths. The Russians gave up attempts to match the Americans by landing a cosmonaut on the moon and instead began to develop space stations. Their first – *Salyut 1* – was

'I believe that this nation should commit itself to achieving the goal, before this decade is out, of landing a man on the Moon, and returning him safely to Earth. No single space project in this period will be more exciting, or more impressive to mankind, or more important to the long-range exploration of space; and none will be so difficult or expensive to accomplish.'

President Kennedy in a speech to Congress, 25 May 1961.

'Since 1965, Russian progress has been slow and over-cautious – the classic symptoms of bureaucrats in power, and no way to wield a "spearhead of advancing technology".'

From a history of space exploration.

Yuri Gagarin in 1967.

launched in April 1971 and Soyuz–Salyut flights have continued ever since. The Russians keep their Salyut permanently staffed and have had a base in orbit almost continuously since 1974. The Americans launched a 'Skylab' space station in 1973 but have not tried to keep up with the Russians in this area, preferring to concentrate on a reusable spacecraft, the space shuttle.

The Salyut space stations and the space shuttle have been very important to military planning. The Russians and Americans have a series of 'spy-satellites' ringing the earth, and the space shuttle programme was mainly funded by the US Department of Defense in exchange for military control over more than half its flights and satellite launches. The only western competitor to the space shuttle as a satellite launcher has been the European *Ariane* rocket successfully launched from Kourou in French Guiana in June 1981.

These satellite launches have helped to improve our life-style. Telecommunications are now highly advanced and weather satellites have improved forecasting for all countries. This is particularly important to third-world countries like India, which has spent more than $700,000,000 on space flights.

The space shuttle has been the major American space initiative in the 1980s. The first craft, *Columbia*, was reused several times and followed by other craft. One of these, *Challenger*, blew up twelve seconds after launch in January 1986. This led to a halt in shuttle flights.

Source D

The US moon landing, July 1969.

Source E

US space shuttle 'Challenger' exploding in mid-air, 28 January 1986.

Questions

Section A

1 Copy and complete the chart to show who was winning the space race 1957–69.

		First human in space	First orbital flight	First link-up of 3 space-craft in flight	First human on the moon	First perman-ently staffed space station
	Launch of first space-craft					
USA	Explorer 1 1958					
Russia	Sputnik 1 1957					

2 Describe the major achievements in space exploration after 1969.

3 How has space exploration improved everyday life on earth in the 1970s and 1980s?

4 Which of the reasons suggested by President Kennedy (Source A) do you think was the most important in influencing the American decision to undertake a moon landing? Give reasons for your answer.

5 Compare Sources C and D. How do they show that space exploration was closely linked with the race for international prestige?

6 Which of Sources D or E do you think a historian from the future might use to illustrate the story of the US space programme? Explain your choice.

Section B

7 If you were a historian using Source A in a history of the space race, would you find it useful to know the date the speech was made? Give a reason for your answer.

8 Source B is from a history of space exploration. Considering what it says about the Russian space programme, when do you think the book might have been written? Explain your answer.

42

China (ii): The Chinese People's Republic

In many ways the story of the People's Republic of China begins with the 'Long March' in 1934. The Red Army left Kiangsi just before Chiang Kai Shek's Kuomintang (KMT) forces surrounded them. Throughout the 6,000-mile journey they fought off attacks from the Kuomintang and survived natural hazards as well. The Long March has become for the Chinese Communists a most important part of their history. Sources A–C show some of the reasons why.

After surviving the Long March, the Chinese Communists regrouped. During the Second World War they fought against the Japanese invaders and gradually grew stronger. After the defeat of Japan, civil war again broke out between the Communists and the KMT. This time the Communists were victorious and on 1 October 1949 Mao Zedong announced the creation of the People's Republic.

By the late 1950s the old landlords had been destroyed and the countryside was reorganised into 26,000 communes, each containing an average of 25,000 people. The communes were needed to improve all aspects of the Chinese economy and daily life. The peasants would not simply be organised to improve food production; there were to be small commune factories to make things like tools, steel and fertilisers, and the communes also built roads, schools, hospitals and canals. Some of these ideas were successful, but in other ways the changes failed to satisfy the people. Many peasants wanted private plots of ground and their own kitchens which were not allowed by the commune.

Throughout the 1960s and 1970s the Chinese Communists changed their plans to suit their needs. The people were encouraged to be adaptable and not to stick too rigidly to plans. China's Prime Minister Zhou Enlai wanted industry and agriculture to merge in the local communes.

Very often workers, students and professionals from the cities were sent to the countryside to experience life in the communes and peasants who wanted to work in the cities had first to be given permits by the commune committees.

In spite of China's progress, by the mid 1960s Mao was concerned that nothing within China should threaten the development of Communism and so, with the strong support of his Defence Minister, Lin Piao, he launched his little 'Red Book'. The book contained quotations from Mao which emphasised that people should be self-disciplined and

Source A

'Chiachinsan (Great Snow Mountain) is blanketed in eternal snow. There are great glaciers in its chasms and everything is white and silent.

Heavy fogs swirled about us, there was high wind, and half way up it began to rain. As we climbed higher and higher we were caught in a terrible hailstorm and the air became so thin we could hardly breathe. Speech was completely impossible and the cold so dreadful that our breath froze and our hands and lips turned blue. Men and animals staggered and fell into chasms and disappeared for ever. Those who sat down to rest or to relieve themselves froze to death on the spot.'

From 'The Great Road' by Agnes Smedley, 1956.

Source B

'Crossing the Chinghai grasslands was an ordeal.... The water underfoot looked like horses' urine and gave off a smell which made people vomit.... Sometimes there were bottomless pools of mud. If you weren't careful, and took a false step, a man and his horse would sink down....'

From 'The Long March' by Dick Wilson, 1971.

Source C

The Long March proclaims to the world that the Red Army is an army of heroes. It shows two hundred million people of eleven provinces that only the road of the Red Army leads to their liberation. Without the Long March how could the masses have known so quickly that there are such great ideas in the world as are upheld by the Red Army?'

From 'The Selected Works of Mao Zedong', Vol.1.

self-critical. In 1966, with the encouragement of his wife Chiang Ch'ing, Mao started the **Cultural Revolution**. Bands of students were organised as 'Red Guards'. A million young people, mostly aged 15 to 19, were brought to camp in Peking and armed with their little Red Books. Schools were closed so that new lessons could be worked out and for two years parades of young Red Guards marched and chanted slogans against Chinese officials who were regarded as unreliable Communists. The young Chinese became fanatical in their task of rooting out people who didn't support the cause and traitors.

Even Zhou Enlai was criticised. Party leaders, generals, professors and all sorts of officials were led through the streets with dunces' hats on their heads and many were later arrested and imprisoned or sent to the countryside. Mao said:

'We must drive actors, poets, dramatists and writers out of the cities and push them all off to the countryside. They should periodically go down in batches to the villages and to the factories.... Whoever does not go down will get no dinner; only when they go down will they be fed.'

After Mao's death in 1976 the damaging effects of the Cultural Revolution were reversed. Mao's wife and three other top communist party officials were branded 'The Gang of Four' and were imprisoned. In the late 1970s and 1980s China began a policy of greater cooperation with the West. For example, agreement was reached with Britain in 1986 about the future of Hong Kong which will return to China in 1997. China is now set on a rapid path of modernisation.

Source D

An injured Red Guard, in hospital, is asked about his home and family.

'After thinking for a while, the soldier said: "I have Chairman Mao". Asked where his home was, he replied, "Peking".

When Nien Ssu-wang left for Peking to receive further treatment, his comrades-in-arms came to see him off. The company political instructor said "Comrade Ssu-wang. I hope you will be patient in the hospital and be resolute...". Nien Ssu-wang finished for him this quotation from Chairman Mao: "...fear no sacrifice and surmount every difficulty to win victory".

The young hero's love for and loyalty to Chairman Mao our great leader is boundless. At that crucial moment when people's lives and state property were in danger, he acted according to Chairman Mao's teaching and, by his heroic action, performed a glorious deed of service to the people. Although he was badly injured and his memory impaired, he still remembered Chairman Mao. In his heart is a never-setting red sun – our most respected and beloved great leader Chairman Mao!'

From 'Peking Review', 17 November 1967.

Source E

The Cultural Revolution: cheering Red Guards at a rally in Peking.

Questions

Section A

1 Who was the leader of the Kuomintang? Why did the KMT begin a war against the Communists in 1927?

2 How did the Long March help to preserve Communism in China?

3 Do you think that the Japanese occupation of China in the Second World War played an important part in the story of Chinese Communism?

4 What was the Cultural Revolution?

5 What do you think the Red Guards are holding in Source E?

Section B

6 Why do you think Chinese Communists regard the Long March as so important?

7 How might Mao's experiences before 1949 have led to his support of the Cultural Revolution in the mid 1960s?

8 Study Source D. Why do you think Nien Ssu-wang felt such devotion to Chairman Mao?

43

Vietnam (i): American Involvement

In 1954, the army which controlled the French colony in Indo-China (now called Vietnam) was defeated at Dien Bien Phu by the **Vietminh**, a communist guerilla army. The leader of this army was Ho Chi Minh and he hoped to turn the whole of Vietnam into a communist state. After the French defeat a peace conference in Geneva decided to divide Vietnam. A communist government led by Ho Chi Minh was set up in the North, with its capital in Hanoi. A non-communist government, led by President Diem, controlled the South and had its capital in Saigon. It was agreed that free elections would be held in 1956 to re-unite the country. Meanwhile all foreign troops were to leave.

It soon became clear, however, that the United States would not allow the country to be re-united if this meant the whole country becoming communist. The reasoning behind this was known as the **Domino Theory**. If you stand a series of dominoes in a line and knock one over it will knock the next one over as it falls and so on all down the line. United States politicians and generals believed that a similar thing could happen with countries. If they allowed one country to become communist another soon would, and eventually the majority of countries would become communist. This Domino Theory was the key to many foreign policy decisions the Americans made.

In the USA President Truman had been followed as president in November 1952 by General Dwight Eisenhower. Eisenhower was popular as the Supreme Allied Commander who had won victory against the Germans in the Second World War and he was expected to take a strong line against Communists. One of Eisenhower's first actions was to appoint a new Secretary of State, John Foster Dulles, who believed that Communism was wicked and immoral. Dulles believed in the principle of 'massive retaliation', that is, if the Communists threatened the USA or any free countries they should be confronted by massive force and, if necessary, the threat of nuclear war. Eisenhower and Dulles were determined to prevent the Domino Theory becoming a reality in Asia and the Far East. By September 1954, they had created an anti-communist alliance – the South East Asia Treaty Organisation (Source E).

In South Vietnam President Diem was not respected by the people. He placed many of his family in important government positions and relied on propaganda to make himself popular in the cities but ignored the countryside. The

'The loss of any single country in South East Asia could lead to the loss of all Asia, then India and Japan, finally endangering the security of Europe.... You have a row of dominoes set up, you knock over the first one and what will happen to the last one is a certainty, that it will go over very quickly.'

President Eisenhower.

Vietnam

Source B

'The path taken by the Chinese people is the path that should be taken by the peoples of the various colonial and semi-colonial countries in their fight for national independence and people's democracy.... This is the way of Mao Zedong.'

Liu Shao-ch'i, one of Mao's advisers and later President of China.

American Central Intelligence Agency (CIA) decided that the USA must intervene in Vietnam if the Diem government was not to be overthrown. The military arm of the Vietminh in the south – the **Vietcong** – was ready to launch attacks and so in 1955, American *advisers* were sent to lead the South Vietnamese army. The elections promised for 1956 were postponed.

Source C

'After 18 May 1955, the date on which all Vietminh forces were supposedly withrawn from the South, the Communists continued to exercise authority in many rural areas. They had extensively infiltrated the civil service, the police and armed forces, and they enjoyed considerable support of the rural population.'

William Henderson, a United States newspaper reporter in Vietnam.

Source D

'Public adulation of the President has reached startling proportions. A constant barrage of propaganda is laid down through the controlled press and radio. "Spontaneous" demonstrations are staged with distressing frequency.''

William Henderson.

Source E

South East Asia Treaty Organisation (SEATO)

The Preamble to the Treaty says that its aim is:

'to uphold the principle of equal rights and self determination of peoples; to promote self-government and to secure the independence of all countries whose peoples desire it and are able to undertake its responsibilities; to continue to co-operate in the economic, social and cultural fields in order to promote higher living standards, economic progress, and social well-being in this region; and to prevent or counter by appropriate means any attempt in the treaty area to subvert their freedom, or to destroy their sovereignty or territorial integrity.'

The treaty was signed by the USA, France, Great Britain, Australia, New Zealand, Thailand, Pakistan and the Philippines.

Questions

Section A

1   Explain in your own words the following terms:
    a   Domino Theory.
    b   massive retaliation.
    c   Vietminh.
    d   Vietcong.

2   What happened in Vietnam in 1954?

3   a   Why was the United States government disturbed about how unpopular President Diem's government was?
    b   What did the United States government do about this?

Section B

4   Does Source B suggest the Domino Theory was right?

5   Study sources B and C. How did the Vietminh copy 'the way of Mao Zedong'?

6   a   Would you expect an American reporter to be biased in favour of or against the South Vietnamese Government?
    b   Which words or phrases in Source D suggest that William Henderson had little faith in President Diem's government? Explain your choice.
    c   Consider your answers to questions 6a and 6b. Do you think Henderson is a reliable source?

7   What do you think President Eisenhower meant when he used the word *'loss'* of any single country (Source A)?

44

Vietnam (ii): War and the Failure of Containment

Source B

'North Vietnam's commitment to seize control of the South is no less total than the commitment of the regime in North Korea in 1950.'

US Defense Department Statement, 1965.

Source C

A Vietnamese child badly burned by American napalm bombing.

The USA wanted President Diem to increase the power of his government and to destroy the Vietcong. It hoped that President Diem would unite all the South Vietnamese anti-communists in his government. Diem, however, could not accept any criticism or opposition, even if it was non-communist. His government became more and more unpopular and his attempts to destroy the Vietcong were so clumsily handled that they actually increased support for the Vietcong in the countryside (Source A).

By 1960 the Vietcong were waging a successful guerilla war against Diem's forces. The USA, now led by President Kennedy, decided to send more military 'advisers' to South Vietnam. Within a year there were over 15,000 American troops helping the South Vietnamese army fight the Vietcong. President Kennedy's successor, Lyndon B. Johnson, was equally determined to support South Vietnam and decided to increase US military involvement.

President Johnson's decision was influenced by several factors. In the summer of 1963 President Diem had been overthrown and shot by his own army. The USA was therefore no longer keen to be supporting an unpopular government. In August 1964 North Vietnamese torpedo boats attacked an American destroyer in the Gulf of Tongking. In the outcry that followed, Johnson was able to persuade the US Congress to support and finance massive US intervention. By 1965 the USA was fighting a full-scale war. Hundreds of thousands of troops and their equipment were poured into Vietnam and the American government

Source A

'Man-hunts involved searches and raids, arrest of suspects, plundering, interrogations sometimes involving torture (even of innocent people), deportation and regrouping of population suspected of intelligence with the rebels.

The communists, finding themselves hunted down, began to fight back. Informers were sought out and shot in increasing numbers, and village chiefs were frequently treated in the same way.'

A description of President Diem's anti-Vietcong campaign.

made it quite clear that it saw the war as one to contain Communism in Indo-China.

The Americans began to bomb North Vietnam openly from 1965 and this led to an increase in the fighting in the South. The Vietcong transported supplies to the South along the Ho Chi Minh trail close to the Cambodian border. The Americans attacked the trail using special bombs intended to destroy the jungle and tree cover. This policy of defoliation was one of several which led to severe criticism of American tactics. Another was the use of napalm (petrol/chemical bombs) against civilian targets. The Vietcong could often hide from the American troops and ambush them. Napalm burned huge areas of the countryside to clear out the Vietcong but often inflicted hideous burns on civilians.

Opposition to the war led to peace protests in the USA. Many parents were against their sons going to war. The public were outraged by the injuries to, and the occasional massacres of, innocent Vietnamese civilians. But most of all young people protested and demonstrated, both against the war itself and the draft law which forced many young men to go and fight in it against their will.

Negotiations to try to end the war began in Paris. US President Nixon was elected in 1968. He announced that he wanted to achieve peace with honour. The Americans did not want to appear to be defeated, but it was not until January 1973 that peace was agreed.

The war had cost the Americans a great deal of money, lives and prestige. Le Duc Tho, a North Vietnamese peace negotiator, described the result as: 'The crowning of thirteen years of valiant struggle which the Vietnamese people have conducted against American imperialism and a group of traitors in the country'. Vietnam was finally unified under a single government in 1975. Communist victory was complete and the policy of containment had failed.

Source D

'Hey, hey, LBJ! How many kids did you kill today?'

Slogan chanted in many anti-war demonstrations in the United States.

Questions

Section A

1 Copy and complete the time-line of events for the Vietnam War.

   1959—Vietcong guerilla war begins to be successful.
   1961
   1963
   1964
   1965
   1968
   1973
   1975

2 Explain the American thinking behind the decision to escalate the war after 1964.

3 Do you think the Americans were fighting on behalf of the Vietnamese?

Section B

4 If the US government was right to denounce the Communists as dedicated to 'the enslavement of free peoples', how do you explain the growth of popularity of the Communists in the South during the war?

5 President Nixon claimed that the US had achieved 'Peace with Honour' in Vietnam. How do you think the following reacted to this claim?

   a The Vietcong
   b American soldiers
   c The South Vietnamese
   d The American public

45

The United States Presidency

'The most powerful man on earth' is the description often given of the President of the United States. Since the Second World War the USA has been the leading power in the West and its President has wielded enormous power and influence. President Truman had the ultimate power in the decision to drop the atomic bomb on Japan in 1945 just as Ronald Reagan has the power in the late 1980s to decide on the 'Star Wars' programme. There have been eight American presidents since 1945 and on three occasions the office of President has gone through a period of crisis.

The first crisis was the assassination of President John F. Kennedy in November 1963. Kennedy was visiting Dallas, Texas, in an open-top car when he was shot dead. Lee Harvey Oswald was arrested for shooting him but before Oswald could stand trial and as he was being moved from police headquarters, he was murdered by Jack Ruby.

For many Americans, the Vietnam war was a betrayal of American idealism. The sufferings of the Vietnamese people and the high death toll turned world opinion against the USA and its President. The Republican candidate, Richard Nixon, was elected in November 1968 and, although his Presidency started badly, his handling of the economy in the early 1970s and his visits to China and Russia made him appear statesmanlike (Source B). But the image of President Nixon was to be shattered by the 'Watergate scandal'. The scandal began in June 1972 with a break-in at the Democratic Party's headquarters in the Watergate building in Washington. The Democrats claimed that the Republican party was responsible and at first Richard Nixon claimed to have no knowledge of the break-in (Source C). Despite Nixon's denials that he was involved, tape recordings which he had made of conversations in the White House with his aides proved that he had lied and the USA entered another crisis. In August 1974, Nixon resigned.

Many Americans were shaken by the admission that a President could be a liar and a cheat. Nixon's successor, Gerald Ford, lost to Jimmy Carter in the November 1986 election. Carter promised an 'open Presidency'. His sincerity and honesty were never questioned, but he was seen as a weak President unable to deal with Russia over Afghanistan and with the hostage crisis in Iran. In 1980 he suffered the humiliation of failing to gain a second term in office and Ronald Reagan became President.

Reagan was instantly popular with the American people because of his strong line against Communism and

Source A

'Kennedy's death shocked the nation, but in a way his death was more important than his life. As President he had shown a determination to tackle problems head-on. The Cuban missile crisis and support for the Civil Rights Movement are just two examples of his idealism. His death evoked great sympathy for the office of President and enabled his successor, Lyndon Johnson, to push through laws and reforms to create his promised "Great Society". The American people now expected great things from their President and the world expected statesmanship.'

A historian's assessment, 1986.

Source B

'Suddenly, he looked like a diplomatic giant, capable of talking in firm but friendly terms to the leaders of the world's most powerful communist states. In the Presidential election of November 1972 he beat George McGovern by a huge margin of forty-seven million to twenty-nine million votes.'

An assessment of President Nixon by Tony Howarth in 'Twentieth Century History'.

Source C

'There had been an effort to conceal the facts both from the public, from you, and from me.... The easiest course would be for me to blame those whom I delegated the responsibility to run the campaign. But that would be a cowardly thing to do.... In any organisation the man at the top must bear the responsibility. I accept it...I must now turn my full attention once again to the larger duties of this office.'

Richard Nixon in a television broadcast to the nation, 30 April 1973.

Source D

REAGAN IN CRISIS MOVE

Following a 21 per cent drop in his popularity President Reagan yesterday requested the appointment of a Watergate-style special prosecutor to investigate the Iran arms affair. He also urged Congress to form a single committee of inquiry. At the same time he appointed Mr Frank Carlucci, a man credited with helping to save Portugal from a Communist takeover, as the new Presidential National Security Adviser to replace Admiral John Poindexter.

ARMS DEAL SILENCE BY NORTH

Lt. Col. Oliver North, dismissed from the National Security Council for his part in the Iran arms sales affair, was reported yesterday to have taken the Fifth Amendment at a hearing of the Senate Intelligence Committee. 'Taking the Fifth' means he refused to testify under the terms of the Fifth Amendment of the US Constitution that protects witnesses from self-incrimination. It was widely used during Watergate. All Washington is now asking whether North will continue to be the silent 'fall guy' like Gordon Liddy in the Watergate affair, or whether he will become a 'squealer' like former Nixon aide John Dean.

From the 'Daily Telegraph', 3 December 1986.

Source E

PRESIDENTIAL DUTY

As events unfold, so the discomfort of those responsible for America's foreign policy increases. America's crisis springs from increasing evidence that foreign policy for this area of the Middle East [the Gulf] was non-existent. Worse, America's strategy has been uninformed, unco-ordinated and uncontrolled. The CIA, the National Security Council and the State Department worked as the spirit moved them. Nobody knew what the other was doing. Improvement can only come from the President himself. The vast apparatus of government in America has to be delegated. Direction of that government, the vision and the impulse lie with the President himself.

Editorial comment in the 'Daily Telegraph', 17 December 1986.

international terrorism. His determination to pursue a policy of negotiation from strength led to renewed arms control talks with Russia and American intervention in Central America and the Caribbean. However, his support of right-wing rebels in Nicaragua called Contras led to a new presidential crisis in November 1986 when it was revealed that arms had been sold to Iran – despite an embargo against this – to secure the release of American hostages. The crisis deepened when it was found that White House officials had used the funds raised from the Iranian arms sales to help the Contras without the knowledge or approval of Congress. The investigations which followed tried to find out if the President had known about the arrangements. The crisis was likened to a second Watergate and was called 'Irangate'.

Source F

The summit meeting in Geneva between Ronald Reagan and Mikhail Gorbachev, November 1985.

Questions

Section A

1 In what years did the following events take place?
  a The assassination of John F. Kennedy
  b Watergate c Irangate

2 Which of the following do you think the American public has looked for most of all in their Presidents since 1945? Explain your answer.

  ● Idealism ● Honesty
  ● Successful dealings with communist countries
  ● Successful management of the domestic economy

Section B

3 Source A is a secondary source. How could you check whether the historian's judgement of President Kennedy is reliable?

4 According to Source B Nixon appeared at one stage as a 'diplomatic giant'. What had he done to earn this title?

5 What happened to change history's judgement of Nixon?

6 In what ways is Source C a statement of the importance of the Presidency? Why was it ironic that President Nixon should be the one to make the statement?

7 Compare Sources D and E. Why do you think the term 'Irangate' was coined by the media?

8 In what ways does Source E show the importance of the Presidency to the whole world?

46

Russia and Eastern Europe (ii): Czechoslovakia, 1968

I n January 1968, the Secretary of the Communist party in Czechoslovakia, Antonin Novotny, was replaced by Alexander Dubcek. The Czechs hoped for an improvement in living standards and a relaxation of the tight control which the Communist party had exercised under Novotny's leadership.

The new Secretary, Dubcek, announced that Czechoslovakia would not be leaving the Warsaw Pact or COMECON. He also announced, however, that he would begin a programme of reforms to improve the lives of ordinary Czechs. It would be a new 'Czechoslovak Road to Socialism'. The reforms were to give greater freedom:

- Press censorship was to be abolished. This had never happened in any communist country before.
- The National Assembly was to be revived and given real powers and responsibilities so that not every decision was taken by the central committee of the Communist Party.
- The idea of allowing opposition parties was to be considered.
- The power and activities of the police were to be reduced.

In Russia, the General Secretary of the Communist Party, Leonid Brezhnev, was alarmed by what was happening in Czechoslovakia. Early in 1968 Albania had withdrawn from the Warsaw Pact, and now it seemed that the alliance was being further weakened by Dubcek's reforms. He was not convinced that Czechoslovakia wished to remain a loyal ally. More importantly, the Russians were afraid that if the Czechs had too much freedom then other 'satellite' countries would begin to make similar reforms and the Warsaw Pact might be weakened.

The Russians tried to get Dubcek to change his policies. In the spring and summer of 1968 a series of actions eventually led to Russian, East German, Polish, Bulgarian and Hungarian troops invading Czechoslovakia.

At first the Czechs did not try to stop the invasion. The Russians sent 500.000 troops into Czechoslovakia to police the country and it was this that provoked the Czechs to resist by fighting and sabotage.

Eventually Dubcek was replaced by a leader acceptable to

Source A

'When forces that are hostile to Socialism try to turn the development of some Socialist country towards Capitalism the suppression of these counter-revolutionary forces becomes not only a problem of the country concerned, but a common problem and concern of all Socialist countries.'

Statement of Leonid Brezhnev: 'The Brezhnev Doctrine', August 1968.

Events of the Summer of 1968

May   Russian military manoeuvres took place in Poland near the Czech frontier.

June–July   Warsaw Pact exercises took place in Czechoslovakia.

Mid-July   Russia, Poland, East Germany, Hungary and Bulgaria sent representatives to a meeting in Warsaw. They issued the Warsaw letter which asked Dubcek to 'suppress anti-socialist forces' in Czechoslovakia.

End of July   Czech and Russian leaders met at Gerna to discuss the situation.

Beginning August   The representatives of Russia, Poland, East Germany, Hungary, Bulgaria and Czechoslovakia met at Bratislava. Dubcek agreed that Czechosolvakia would remain a loyal member of the Warsaw Pact and Brezhnev agreed that Czechoslovakia could follow its own domestic policy.

Mid-August   President Tito of Yugoslavia and President Ceaușescu of Rumania visited Dubcek and gave him their support.

21 August   The Russians invaded. Dubcek was arrested and taken to Moscow.

the Russians, and the liberal reforms were at an end. There had been many protests against the Russian invasion – Rumania had condemned it as a 'flagrant violation of the national sovereignty of a socialist country'. Jan Palach, a Czech student, had set fire to himself in the centre of Prague. The United States and other western governments made official protests to the Russians. But none of this changed the situation in Czechoslovakia. The Russians and the Americans had signed a nuclear non-proliferation treaty in July and the West was not prepared to abandon hopes of future improved relations for the sake of the Czechs.

As a protest against the Russian invasion of his country a Czech student, Jan Palach, poured petrol over himself and burned himself to death in the main square of Prague. Thousands of Czechs turned out to watch his funeral procession.

Source C

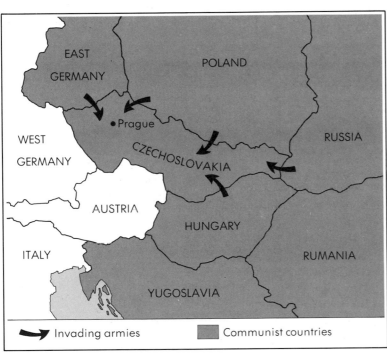

The invasion of Czechoslovakia.

Source B

A street cartoon seen in Prague during the Russian invasion.

Questions

Section A

1 Describe the reforms introduced by Dubcek.

2 Study the map. Do you think the Russians would have been worried if Czechoslovakia had left the Warsaw Pact?

3 Dubcek said Czechoslovakia would not leave the Warsaw Pact. Why else were the Russians worried about Czech reforms?

4 Did the Russians give Dubcek any warning that they would not accept his reforms?

5 Why do you think the Russians were always keen to be seen to be acting with other Warsaw Pact countries?

Section B

6 What feelings do you think the artist of Source B intended to provoke?

7 The death of Jan Palach was widely reported.

   a How do you think Czechs in Prague felt when they heard about it?

   b How do you think the Russian soldiers in Prague felt about it?

   c How do you think people in the West felt when they heard about it?

47

Russia and Eastern Europe (iii): The Suppression of Polish 'Solidarity'

On 13 December 1981, General Wojciech Jaruzelski announced a state of emergency in Poland and the introduction of military government and martial law (Source A). What had brought about this situation in Poland? Since 1956 Poland had been a close ally of Russia. First Wladyslaw Gomulka (1956–70) and then Edward Gierek (1970–80) had led the communist government in Poland. Any unrest, such as food riots in 1968 or meat riots in 1976, had been harshly put down.

In 1980, however, the Poles rebelled against poor economic management which had led to high prices and shortages of most goods. Strikes broke out throughout the country. The first was by the Gdansk shipyard workers who demanded the right to strike, free trade unions, more power for the Catholic Church and the release of political prisoners.

The strike committee formed a trade union called **Solidarnösc** (Solidarity), led by Lech Walesa, and the union rapidly grew into a nationwide movement with more than 10,000,000 members. Many members of the Communist party also joined and Russia became alarmed that the communist system in Poland was under threat. Lech Walesa described the reason for the Solidarity movement as being a loss of faith in the ability of the government to manage the economy properly. Solidarity never organised an armed attempt to overthrow the government. It worked to persuade the government to make concessions step by step.

At first Solidarity seemed to be succeeding. In August 1980, Deputy Prime Minister Jagielski and Lech Walesa signed the Gdansk agreement which gave the strikers the right to set up an independent trade union, and in September Gierek fell from power. In December 1980, Russia, anxious not to intervene because of hostile world opinion about its invasion of Afghanistan, called an Eastern Bloc summit in Moscow. A statement was issued that Poland could solve its own problems.

In February 1981 General Jaruzelski became Prime Minister of Poland but was at first unable to stop the progress of Solidarity. So alarmed were the Russians that in June 1981 they sent a letter to the central committee of the Polish

Source A

'I address you today as a soldier and as the leader of the Polish government. I address you on a matter of the utmost importance. Our country is on the edge of the abyss. Achievements of many generations, raised from the ashes, are collapsing into ruin. State structures no longer function.

I declare that today a Military Council for National Salvation has been established. The Council of State, in accordance with the Polish constitution, has declared martial law as from midnight in all of Poland. I want everybody to understand the motives and the aims of this action. We are not striving for a military takeover, a military dictatorship. The nation is strong and wise enough to develop a democratic system of socialist government....

At this difficult moment I turn to our Socialist allies and friends. We value their confidence and constant help. The Polish–Soviet alliance is and will remain the cornerstone of the Polish *raison d'etat* and the guarantee of inviolability of our borders. Poland is and will be a firm link of the Warsaw Pact, an unfailing member of the Socialist community.

Fellow-countrymen, before the whole world I want to repeat these immortal words: "Poland is not yet lost as long as we live".'

General Jaruzelski, 13 December 1981.

Source B

'Is it any wonder that people are in despair? They must begin queuing outside the butchers' shops early in the morning and may still find there is no meat to buy with their ration books.

We want to achieve a free trade-union movement which will allow workers to manage the economy through joint-control with the government.'

Interview with Lech Walesa, July 1981.

Communist party complaining of the 'flexibility' of the Polish government. In September major Warsaw Pact manoeuvres began alongside Poland's eastern border. It seemed that Russia was ready to intervene once again in one of its satellite countries but it still held back, even when Solidarity called on other workers in East European countries 'to follow the difficult path of fighting for a free trade-union movement'. In mid-September the Russians called on the Polish government to take 'prompt steps to deal with the anti-Soviet campaign' in Poland.

In October, General Jaruzelski replaced Kania as first secretary of the Communist party and soldiers were sent into the countryside to 'organise supplies'. Solidarity organised a wave of strikes in response and, despite appeals from Lech Walesa for restraint, the strikes continued. In November, the government announced a ban on strikes and on 13 December General Jaruzelski proclaimed martial law. Polish troops moved into the centre of all major cities.

In 1982, the Polish government continued its attack on Solidarity. Several leaders were interned, others went 'underground' and Lech Walesa was taken into and out of custody and warned about his future behaviour. Anyone who distributed leaflets or who caused disturbances could be punished, and workers were not allowed to go on strike. Anyone who wanted to give up his or her job had to go before a military tribunal, and the authorities could take any action 'in the interest of safeguarding public safety'. Some observers compared the situation to the harsh style of government in the Eastern Europe of the early 1950s.

Questions

Section A

1 What part did the following play in the story of Solidarity?
   a the Gdansk shipyard
   b food shortages
   c Lech Walesa
   d General Jaruzelski

2 How was Solidarity a threat to the Soviet system?

3 Why do you think that Russia did not intervene in Poland to crush Solidarity?

Section B

4 Is Source A a reliable source for a historian trying to explain the suppression of Solidarity? Give reasons for your answer.

5 Is Source C a useful source for a historian trying to explain the suppression of Solidarity? Give reasons for your answer.

6 Does Source C help you to decide whether Source B is reliable?

7 Source D shows Polish soldiers and tanks in the streets of Gdansk. Does this show that Poland had solved its own problems?

Source C

A queue outside a Polish meat shop.

Source D

Polish tanks in the streets of Gdansk following the announcement of martial law.

48

The Middle East (i): The Creation of Israel

In November 1917, the British Foreign Secretary, A.J. Balfour, wrote to a leading Zionist, Lord Rothschild, telling him that the British government believed that a national home for the Jews should be created in Palestine (Source A). Why was this letter important? Who were the Zionists, and where was Palestine?

The Zionists were a group founded in 1897 by an Austrian journalist, Theodore Herzl, who believed it was essential that the Jews should have a homeland of their own. Many believed this should be in Palestine because of the Jews' history and the fact that the Old Testament makes it clear that it was the land promised to the Jews by God.

Palestine, by the nineteenth century, was an Arab land ruled by the Turks. However, after Turkey was defeated as an ally of Germany in the First World War, the Turkish Empire was split up. The League of Nations gave Palestine and most of the Middle East to Britain and France to administer. This did not please the Arabs because during the war they had fought for the British against the Turks and believed that they had been promised self-government and an Arab state at the end of it (Source C).

Clearly, the British had made contradictory statements to both Arabs and Jews and both were expecting Palestine as a homeland. Tension between Arabs and Jews in Palestine became serious during the period of British rule. In 1914 there had been 83,000 Jews living in Palestine and by 1936 the number had gone up to 400,000. The first major outbreak of violence happened in 1929 after a Jewish boy was stabbed to death. His funeral turned into a riot which spread throughout the main towns, including Jerusalem and Hebron.

The Arabs resented Jewish immigration into Palestine and blew up bridges and trains. The Arabs were determined to drive out the British while they (the Arabs) still outnumbered the Jews. They wanted an independent Arab state.

After Hitler came to power the British found it very difficult to solve the problem. The persecution of Jews in Germany meant many more Jews wanted to emigrate to Palestine, but as war came near the British knew they would need the Arabs' loyalty if they were to defend their bases in the Middle East and the Suez Canal. The British needed to maintain their supply-lines of oil. To please the Arabs the British government announced in a White Paper of 1939 that for the next five years only 75,000 Jewish immigrants would be allowed to enter Palestine and afterwards more Jews

Source A

The Balfour Declaration, 1917.

Source B

Some events in the history of the Jewish people, AD 70–1948

AD 70 – Jewish state in Palestine collapses after revolt against the Romans
1096 – Attacks made on Jews in France and the Rhineland by Crusaders going to the Holy Land
1480–92 – Spanish Inquisition persecutes Jews – thousands die at the stake
1881 – Pogroms (attacks against Jews) begin in Russia
1881–1914 – 3 million Jews flee from eastern Europe because of persecution
1917 – Balfour Declaration
1933–45 – Persecution of Jews in Germany
1948 – Founding of the State of Israel

would only be admitted with Arab agreement. The Jews campaigned in Palestine and the USA for unlimited immigration.

After the Second World War there was much sympathy for the Jews as what had happened in the concentration camps became known (see pages 58-9). A Jewish terrorist group tried to drive the British out of Palestine, and there was also violence between Jews and Arabs. In February 1947 Britain announced it would ask the United Nations to decide what should happen to Palestine, and in November the UN decided it should be split in two – into a Jewish homeland and an Arab homeland. The Jews accepted this and, in May 1948 (when the British left), proclaimed the state of Israel, but the Arabs refused to agree. Neighbouring Arab states joined with the Palestinian Arabs in a war to destroy Israel. By the end of the year Israel had fought off these attacks and captured some of the territory the UN had said should go to the Arabs. At the end of the war Israel refused to give back the captured territory to the Arabs and the Arab states refused to accept that Israel had a right to exist.

Source C

'Great Britain is prepared to recognize and support the independence of the Arabs in all the region. Great Britain will guarantee the Holy Places against all external aggression. When the situation admits Great Britain will give the Arabs her advice and will assist them to establish the most suitable forms of government.

I am convinced that this declaration will assure you beyond all possible doubt the sympathy of Great Britain towards the aspirations of her friends the Arabs.'

From a letter from McMahon, a British diplomat, to Sherif Hussein, the Arab leader in Palestine, 1916.

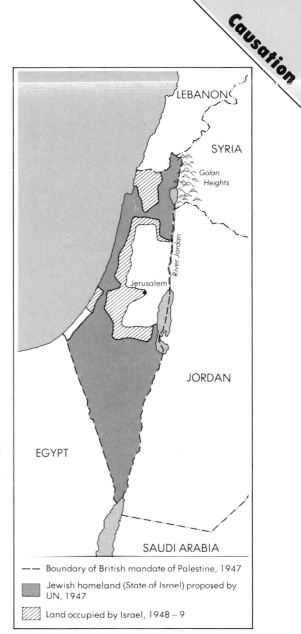

-- -- Boundary of British mandate of Palestine, 1947

▓ Jewish homeland (State of Israel) proposed by UN, 1947

▨ Land occupied by Israel, 1948 – 9

Palestine in 1948.

Questions

Section A

1 What do you think a 'homeland' is?

2 a Why do you think the Arabs wanted to set up a state in Palestine?
  b What encouragement did they receive from the British?

3 a Why do you think the Jews wanted to set up a state in Palestine?
  b What encouragement did they receive from the British?

4 What events between 1900 and 1947 may have increased the desire of a the Jews b the Arabs to set up a 'homeland' in Palestine?

Section B

5 What were the short-term causes of the following?
  a The Jewish demand for emigration to Palestine in the 1930s

  b Arab–Jewish fighting in Palestine in the 1930s
  c British immigration policy into Palestine 1939–45
  d Jewish attacks on British troops 1945–7

6 How do your answers to question 6 reveal a chain of causation? Can you trace the chain further forwards or backwards in time? Give examples to illustrate your answer.

7 What reasons can you think of which might have caused the super-powers to be interested in the Middle East after 1948?

49

The Middle East (ii): Suez

A revolution took place in Egypt in July 1952. A group of army officers who were discontented with the rule of King Farouk forced him to abdicate and declared Egypt to be a republic. One of these officers, Gamal Abdul Nasser, became President of Egypt in 1956 and promised to improve Egypt. In particular he wanted to improve standards of living and to redistribute land more fairly.

Egypt was a country dependent on irrigation and water from the River Nile, and one of the ways Nasser tried to improve it was to build the Aswan Dam. This would increase water supplies and therefore improve agriculture and also provide hydro-electricity. However, Nasser needed money to build the dam and the Americans used their

Source A

'The income of the Suez Canal in 1955 amounted to £35,000,000. In return for the 120,000 Egyptians who perished digging it and for the money spent on building it, we get £1,000,000.

The Suez Canal Company sitting in Paris is a usurping company. It usurped our concessions... We shall build the High Dam and we shall gain our usurped rights. We shall build the High Dam as we desire. We are determined. The Canal Company annually takes £35,000,000. Why shouldn't we take it ourselves?...

As I told you a little while ago, it is no shame to be poor and to strive and build my country. What is shameful, however, is to suck blood. They sucked our blood, and extorted and stole our rights. Today as we retrieve these rights, I declare on behalf of the Egyptian people that we shall preserve these rights and cherish them. We shall protect these rights because thereby we shall be making up for the past. Today, O citizens, the Suez Canal has been nationalised... Today, O citizens, we declare that our property has been returned to us. The rights about which we were silent have been restored to us. Today, citizens, with the annual income of the Suez Canal amounting to £35,000,000...we shall not look for...American aid... Your Egyption brethren... have started to take over the Canal Company and its property and to control shipping through the Canal – the Canal which is owned by Egypt.'

The announcement of the nationalisation of the Suez Canal Company by President Nasser on 26 July 1956.

Source B

'The full responsibility for the aggressive actions against Egypt falls on the governments of England, France and Israel. The whole world sees now the worthlessness of their promises, their false support for the cause of peace, their hypocritical declarations that they are concerned about the freedom and independence of nations.'

From 'Pravda', 2 November 1956.

Source C

'The President is authorised to assist any Middle Eastern nation in the development of economic strength to maintain its independence. The President is authorised to offer military assistance to any nation of that area desiring such assistance. The USA regards the independence of the nations in the Middle East as vital to its interest and world peace. To this end the United States is prepared to use armed force to assist any nation against armed aggression from any country controlled by international communism.'

From the 'Eisenhower Doctrine' – a resolution of the United States Senate, 9 March 1957.

The Suez Canal

influence with the World Bank to refuse Egypt a loan. This was because they believed Nasser was too friendly with the Russians and their allies. For example, in 1955 Egypt had bought arms from Czechoslovakia.

Nasser decided that the only way to obtain the money was by seizing the Suez Canal. On 26 July 1956 Nasser announced the nationalisation of the Canal (Source A).

The seizure of the Canal worried the western allies who needed Middle East Oil which came to Western Europe through the Suez Canal. Britain and France were particularly concerned as the main interesed parties in the Canal. The British Prime Minister, Anthony Eden, said Nasser would not be allowed 'to have his thumb on our windpipe'.

The Egyptians had also angered the French by supporting Arab nationalists in the French colony of Algeria, and had angered the Israelis because **Fedayeen** terrorists, who were attacking Israel, had their bases in Egypt. In February 1955 the Israelis had attacked Egyptian military bases in Gaza, and in return Nasser had prevented Israeli ships entering the Gulf of Suez and therefore the Canal. Israel took advantage of Nasser's decision to nationalise the Canal and invaded Egypt on 29 October 1956.

The British and French had secretly agreed to back Israel and were waiting to intervene to demand that both sides withdraw from the Canal zone. The Israelis rapidly occupied the Sinai Peninsula and on 30 October the British and French issued an ultimatum that both sides withdraw to positions 10 miles on each side of the Canal. When the Egyptians refused, British and French aircraft began bombing Egypt, and British and French paratroops and seaborne forces landed in and around Port Said. Egypt retaliated by sinking ships to block the Canal.

It was at this point that the super-powers intervened. Russia was the first to do so, threatening to come to Egypt's aid. The Americans were alarmed that the Russians might carry out their threat of rocket attacks. They told Britain and France that oil supplies would be cut off unless they withdrew their forces, and so a cease-fire was agreed on 6 November, followed by a gradual withdrawal. The British and French troops were replaced by a UN peace-keeping force. Israel agreed to withdraw its troops from Sinai in 1957.

The war had been humiliating for Britain and France because they had been forced to back down. It had angered the Americans because it strengthened ties between Egypt and Russia and increased Russian prestige in the eyes of the Arab countries. The Israeli army had defeated the Egyptians but although they had destroyed much of the Egyptian army's arms and equipment these were quickly built up again by the Russians. The main gain for the Israelis was the reaffirmation of American support for Israel which came in the Eisenhower Doctrine of March 1957 (Source C).

Questions

Section A

1 Copy out the following paragraph, choosing one of the alternatives in brackets.

Many quarrels came to a head at Suez in 1956. Egypt nationalised the Suez Canal because it needed money. Also the new government of Egypt (wanted to build national pride/didn't like the French and British). Britain and France were involved because they (owned the Suez Canal Company/were in power in Palestine) and they also depended on the oil which came through the Suez Canal. Israel and Egypt had not settled the differences which had led to the war in 1948 and (arguments over which of them owned the Suez Canal/the Fedayeen attacks) were making this worse. Finally, both Russia and the USA were keen to increase their influence in the area. The USA was becoming more closely linked with (Egypt/Israel) while the Russians were closer to (Egypt/Israel).

2 Study Source A. To whom is Nasser referring when he says 'they sucked our blood, and extorted and stole our rights'?

3 Study Source B. What 'hypocritical declarations' do you think the editor of *Pravda* had in mind when he accused the western governments?

Section B

4 **Provenance** is the word historians use to describe where a source has come from. Where do you think **each** of Sources A, B and C has come from?

5 Who do you think was originally intended to read or hear Sources A, B and C? Give reasons for your answers.

6 Do historians need to know both these things (see questions 4 and 5) in order to decide if a source is reliable or not? Explain your answer.

50

The Middle East (iii): The Wars of 1967 and 1973

The Six-Day War

After the Suez conflict Israel and the Arab states continued to increase the size of their armies and weapon stocks with help from the super-powers. The Russians supplied MiG jets, bombers, rockets and tanks to both Egypt and Syria. Israel was able to buy warplanes from the French – the Mystère and the Mirage jets – and received other supplies from the USA.

Israel was being continually attacked by Arab terrorists and particularly by the **Palestine Liberation Movement (Al Fatah)** which had bases in Syria and Jordan, where its members were trained in guerilla tactics. From 1963 Syria directed warlike radio broadcasts against Israel (Source A) and organised artillery bombardments of Israeli villages from the Golan Heights – the mountainous border region.

Eventually, Israel took reprisals for the terrorist attacks and sent warplanes to bomb Syria in April 1967. This action led to Arab demands for war against Israel. President Nasser asked for the UN peace-keeping force, which had been stationed in the Suez area since 1956, to be withdrawn and on 23 May announced that Israeli ships could not enter the Gulf of Suez (Source B).

The Israelis were convinced that the Arab states were going to attack them. Egyptian, Syrian, Jordanian, Iraqi and Kuwaiti troops had all been mobilised and Algeria and Sudan had promised help.

On 5 June 1967 Israel attacked first and turned its main force against Egypt. Within six days the Egyptian air force was almost totally destroyed and Egypt's armies pushed back across the Suez Canal. Jordan was attacked and, despite heavy losses, the Israelis captured the Arab sector of Jerusalem and pushed the Jordanian army back across the River Jordan. The Golan Heights were captured from Syria. The Israeli assault had been planned by General Moshe Dayan, who became Defence Minister on 1 June, four days before the war broke out. It was his careful planning and the use of surprise which had won the war for Israel, but there was no peace treaty. The Arabs agreed to a cease-fire but, when Israel refused to hand back territory captured in the war, the Arabs were determined to fight again in the future.

Source A

'We have decided to drench this land with our blood, to oust you, aggressors, and to throw you into the sea for good.'

From a Syrian radio broadcast before the Six-Day War.

Source B

'The Israeli flag will no longer pass the Gulf of Aqaba; our sovereignty over the Gulf is indisputable. If Israel threatens us with war, we will reply thus, "Go ahead, then".'

President Nasser, 23 May 1967.

Source C

'1. Each nation in the area must have the right to live without threat of attack or extinction.
2. More than a million homeless Arab refugees must be settled justly before a lasting peace can be achieved.
3. Maritime rights must be respected; rights of innocent passage through international waterways must be preserved for all nations.
4. Arms shipments into the area should be reduced and limited on all sides, thus reducing tensions and freeing money for vital economic development.
5. Secure and agreed borders must be set up for all states in the region.'

President Johnson's statement of American policy, 18 June 1967.

The Middle East oil supplies were vitally important to the West and the Six-Day War increased the fears that the conflict might threaten these supplies. The Arab oil-producing states were not happy about America sending supplies to Israel and so President Johnson quickly issued a statement to show the Americans wanted a just settlement for both sides.

The Yom Kippur War

President Nasser died in 1970. Nasser's successor, President Anwar Sadat, expelled Russian advisers in 1972 but continued to plot with Syria a war of revenge against Israel.

On 6 October 1973 most Jews were at prayer in their synagogues because this was Yom Kippur, the Jewish Day of Atonement – an important religious festival. Egypt and Syria chose the day to launch a surprise attack. Egyptian troops crossed the Suez Canal and Syria attacked the Israeli forces in the Golan Heights. The Arab armies had more than a million men and three times as much equipment, planes and tanks as in the Six-Day War but the Israelis managed to counter attack and by 10 October had driven back the Syrians and had marched on towards Damascus. Only a combined resistance by Syrian, Iraqi and Jordanian troops stopped the Israelis going further.

The Egyptians were more difficult to overcome and the Israelis, led by General Sharon, had to land their troops on the Egyptian side of the Canal. Sharon's troops were able to threaten Egyptian supply routes and the road to Cairo and on 25 October a cease-fire was agreed.

The war had several important consequences.

- In 1968 the Arab states had formed OAPEC (Organisation of Arab Petroleum Exporting Countries) and they now announced a 70 per cent increase in the price of oil. This caused an economic crisis in the West.
- The USA ordered a world-wide alert on 24-25 October in case the conflict spread and involved the super-powers.
- The war brought pressure on western countries to seek a solution to the Arab–Israeli conflict.
- The Arabs had failed to force Israel to return to its pre-1967 borders. This left the situation in the area very tense.
- In 1974, the American Secretary of State, Dr Henry Kissinger, arranged for a disengagement of the opposing forces and in 1975 Israel withdrew from part of Sinai in return for Egypt's decision to allow Israeli-bound vessels through the Suez Canal. However, the main Arab grievances, and particularly the Palestinian problem, were not sorted out.

Changes in Israel's borders 1949-74.

Questions

Section A

1 How does the map show that 'the most important result of the Six-Day War was that Israel gained defendable borders'?

2 What part was played in the Six-Day War by the following?
a The super-powers b Terrorism
c Moshe Dayan

3 Describe the Yom Kippur War in your own words. Copy the map and mark on it, using a colour key, the troop movements of the Arab and Israeli armies.

Section B

4 Are the following statements causes of the wars of 1967 and 1973? Give reasons for your answer in each case.
a The super-powers continued to arm the Arabs and Israelis and this made war possible.
b The Arabs hated Israel and were concerned for Palestinian rights.
c Israel attacked Egypt in 1956.

5 a What were the short-term causes of the wars in 1967 and 1973?
b What were the long-term causes?

6 What were the results of the wars?

51

The Middle East (iv): The Palestinians and Conflict in Lebanon

Source A

'We the Palestinian Arab People, who believe in its Arabism and in its right to regain its homeland to realise its freedom and dignity, have determined to move forward on the path of holy war until complete and final victory has been attained.'

From the Palestine National Covenant, 1964.

I n November 1967 the United Nations Security Council passed Resolution 242 which called on Israel and the other parties involved in the Middle East conflict to establish 'just solutions to the refugee problem'. This problem had begun with the creation of the State of Israel in 1948, which had led to the loss of the lands of the Palestinian Arabs. Many of these Arabs took refuge in the Gaza strip and in camps close to Israel's border in neighbouring Arab countries, particularly Jordan. In May 1964, after years of suffering, the Palestinians formed the Palestine Liberation Organisation (PLO) and determined to fight to recover the lands lost in 1948.

After Israel's victory in the Six-Day War of 1967, Arab governments, particularly Egypt, began to give support to the PLO, together with arms to fight a terrorist war against Israel. In the early 1970s, the PLO attracted world-wide attention to their cause through acts of terrorism. The most famous was the murder of members of the Israeli Olympic team in an attack on the Munich Olympic village in 1972. There were also frequent hijackings of aircraft.

The leader of the PLO was Yasser Arafat. He had founded a Palestinian resistance group called Al Fatah (victory) in 1956 and, in 1968, when the Israelis attacked Al Fatah bases in Jordan, Arafat led a successful defence of them. As a result, he was appointed chairman of the PLO and continued to organise guerilla raids against Israel. Arafat became so powerful, and the PLO had attracted so much attention by early 1970, that King Hussein of Jordan decided to expel them before he lost the ability to govern his own country. After being driven out of Jordan in 1971, the PLO concentrated its operations and camps in Lebanon.

In 1974 the PLO was recognised by all the Arab states, including Jordan, as the rightful representative body of the Palestinian people. Arafat persuaded the United Nations to support the claims of the Palestinians and the right of the PLO to be present at peace negotiations. Between 1975 and 1977, civil war broke out in Lebanon between the Christian and Muslim communities. During this war the PLO was able to make itself even stronger, and in the 1980s regular guerilla attacks were launched against Israel from PLO bases in Lebanon. The Lebanese government was so weak that part of

Source B

PLO terrorists celebrate the blowing-up of a hijacked VC10 in 1970.

Source C

The remains of the American Headquarters in Lebanon after Shiites drove lorries packed with explosives into it.

its territory around the Bekaa valley was occupied by Syria. In the summer of 1982, Israel decided that the situation had become unacceptable and invaded Lebanon to drive out the PLO.

Yasser Arafat and his men were driven steadily back until the PLO were pinned down in Beirut. After negotiations the PLO were allowed to leave Beirut with their weapons, but several units disowned Arafat and declared he was no longer leader of the PLO. The invasion was unpopular in Israel especially after the PLO had left Beirut. The Israeli troops which occupied the city did not prevent massacres by Lebanese Christians of the remaining Palestinian refugees in the Sabra and Shatila camps, and in September the Israeli government bowed to pressure from its people to make a phased withdrawal from Lebanon.

As soon as the Israelis began to withdraw, civil war broke out again in Lebanon, with fighting between the Muslim Druze and the Christians. To restore order, the United Nations organised a peace-keeping force early in 1983 and sent in UN troops from the United States, France, Italy and Britain. These units were intended to strengthen the Lebanese government but Syrian troops were still in the country and organised the Muslim groups–the Druze and Shiites–to fight government forces which were dominated by Christians.

The Lebanese government of President Gemayel was only able to control the area around Beirut. To the north, the Druze led by Walid Jumblatt were in control. To the east, Syrian troops were still in the Bekaa valley, and to the south Israeli troops remained in control of the area south of the Awali river. In October 1985, the Shiites launched a suicide attack on the international peace-keeping force and killed 216 Americans and 58 French. Yasser Arafat and 5000 of his supporters had taken refuge in the Baddaui refugee camp in the northern Lebanese town of Tripoli. Early in November, the PLO groups who had deserted Arafat, and who were backed by the Syrians, attacked the Baddaui camp. Arafat and his men were finally forced out of Lebanon by their one-time comrades.

Activity

Sources B and C are both photographs which were used in newspapers. In groups, decide what caption would be used to go with each photograph in the following newspapers:

a an Arab paper supporting Arafat
b an Israeli paper
c an American paper
d a Syrian paper.

Questions

Section A

1 Copy and complete the time-line for the history of the PLO:

1948 – Palestinians lose their lands to newly-created Israel
1956 – Creation of Al Fatah, led by Yasser Arafat
1964 – Formation of the PLO
1967 –
1968 –
1971 –
1974 –
1975 –
1982 –
1983 –

2 According to the Palestine National Covenant (Source A), what three things have caused the Palestinians to wage a 'holy war' against Israel?

3 Which of the following has done most to bring the Palestinian cause to the attention of the world?

a PLO terrorism
b The United Nations
c The actions of Israel

Section B

4 Explain the chain of events which has caused the Palestinians to move their homes since 1948.

	Reason for move
Palestine 1948	
Jordan 1971	
Beirut 1982	
Tripoli 1983	

5 a What was the overall aim of the PLO?
b Why did King Hussein want the PLO out of Jordan?
c Why did Israel invade Lebanon?
d Look again at your answers to a–c. Neither the PLO nor King Hussein nor the Israeli government wanted to destroy peace and law and order in Lebanon. Does this mean that when historians are trying to explain what happened in Lebanon they should not suggest that the actions of these three can have been causes? Give reasons for your answer.

52

The Middle East (v): The Islamic Revolution

All Muslims are expected to obey Islamic Law, but in the 1920s and 1930s the Shah of Persia changed his country's name to the ancient one of Iran, and began a modernisation programme which did away with many Islamic traditions. In 1936, women were forbidden to cover their faces as Islamic custom demanded, and everyone was made to wear European dress. This modernisation programme continued after the Second World War. In January 1979, however, the reigning Shah and his family were forced to flee Iran, and his government was replaced by that of the Muslim Shia leader, the Ayatollah Khomeini.

The situation in the Middle East, the wars with Israel and the Palestinian question had convinced many Muslim Arabs that their main enemy was the West, especially the United States. They thought Americans exploited the Middle East, especially to get cheap oil. In 1973 after the fourth Arab–Israeli war, the Organisation of Arab Petroleum Exporting Countries (OAPEC) had dramatically increased the price of oil as retaliation against the West for its support of Israel. This action also strengthened the popular belief that all things western were to be opposed.

After Ayatollah Khomeini came to power in Iran, revolutionary guards organised the 'round-up' and trial of

Source C

Source B

A demonstration in favour of Ayatollah Khomeini.

Source D

'*27 December 1985* – On the same day and at almost the same time, terrorist attacks of almost unprecedented brutality were carried out at the airports in Rome and Vienna. In Rome a Palestinian suicide squad killed sixteen and injured over seventy. In the twin attack in Vienna three people died and forty were injured.

The terrorists were members of the *Abu Nidal* group.'

From the International Yearbook, 1986.

pro-western sympathisers. These included many supporters of the deposed Shah who were tried by Islamic People's Courts. In particular, members of the Shah's Security Service (SAVAK) were quickly tried and executed. Punishments often seemed brutal to western eyes. For example, in Isfahan two men were shot because they had not allowed a dead opponent of the Shah to be buried according to Islamic tradition.

The Ayatollah's government held a referendum in March 1979 and a large majority voted for the creation of an Islamic Republic in Iran. Iranian women were ordered to dress once again in traditional robes. Relations with the United States were broken off. Arms deals with the USA and France were cancelled, and the Israeli embassy was handed over to the PLO leader, Yasser Arafat, as a symbolic gesture.

The success of the Islamic revolution in Iran led to similar movements throughout the Middle East. Early in 1980, Muslim fanatics occupied the Great Mosque in the holy city of Mecca, in Saudi Arabia, and demanded that Saudi Arabia return to Islamic traditions. Although the revolt was quickly crushed, the calls for Islamic reforms spread to Egypt. Here President Sadat was under pressure to improve the Egyptian economy so that the poor had more chance to make the pilgrimage to Mecca.

From the West's point of view, the results of the Islamic revolution in Iran were alarming. In 1980, war broke out between Iran and Iraq, threatening oil supply routes through the Arabian Gulf. The price of oil reached its highest levels, causing more damage to the western economy. At the beginning of 1979 the US embassy in Tehran had been attacked and fifty-two Americans taken hostage. By 1980, it was clear these hostages were not to be released quickly. In fact, the Iranians threatened to try the hostages on spying charges.

President Carter, desperate to solve the crisis, eventually ordered a commando raid on Iran, but this raid failed badly when a helicopter crashed into a transport plane in the Iranian desert, and eight Americans were killed. This episode seriously weakened President Carter in the eyes of the American people and paved the way for Ronald Reagan's success in the 1981 elections.

The hostages were eventually released in January 1981, but the Islamic revolution has continued to alarm the West. Islamic fundamentalists led a suicide attack on US and French troops in Lebanon (see page 102–3) and terrorist attacks on American citizens throughout the world were seen as being inspired by the Libyan leader, Colonel Ghaddafi, an enthusiastic supporter of the Islamic revolution. In 1986, a US air raid was launched against Libya as a retaliation for these terrorist attacks. Mutual fear and suspicion remain between Islamic fundamentalists and western governments.

Questions

Section A

1 How did the modernisation programme of the Shahs lead to the Iranian revolution of 1979?

2 What caused Muslims throughout the Middle East to turn against the West after 1973?

3 What can you tell about Iran after the Islamic revolution from:
 a the way women dressed?
 b the arms deals with the United States and France?
 c the government's actions over the Israeli embassy?

4 Explain how the Islamic revolution has affected the elections for the Presidency of the United States.

5 Why do you think western governments are so worried about the Islamic revolution?

Section B

6 Source C shows part of an incident described in the text. What do you think it is? Give reasons for your answer.

7 Do you agree with the following statement?

'Source B shows that the Ayatollah Khomeini was popular throughout Iran.'

8 Can you see any connection between Source A and Source D? Explain your answer.

9 Are the sources on these two pages sufficient to prove that the Islamic revolution is widely supported and in conflict with the West?

53

Africa (i): De-colonisation and the Case of Kenya

In the nineteenth century European countries had competed with each other all over the world to build empires. The race for colonies in Africa became known as the 'Scramble for Africa'. Early in the twentieth century only two countries, Liberia and Abyssinia (Ethiopia), were ruled by black Africans (Source A) and this situation remained largely unchanged until after the Second World War when Africans began to demand their independence. In 1945, a Pan African Congress was held in Manchester to discuss decolonisation.

The British had had the largest empire but were no longer able to enforce their rule. Britain needed American help to rebuild its shattered and war-torn economy and the USA was not keen to support the old order of the British Empire. However, Britain did not grant independence to countries straight away and in Africa the process was particularly slow.

The British and French had withdrawn from all their north African colonies (except French Algeria) by 1956, but no black African states, except Ghana (1957) and Guinea (1958), received independence before 1960. The British attitude was that most black African countries were not ready for self-government. Most of the economies were underdeveloped with little industry; only cash crops and minerals could be exported, and agriculture often did not produce enough food for the local population. There were few schools for the African children, and tribal rivalries might lead to civil wars rather than sound political systems.

Black leaders, however, were not prepared to accept these ideas. Many of them believed that these were just British excuses to allow them to continue to exploit Africa's wealth of resources. In Kenya the Kenya Africa Union (KAU), led by Jomo Kenyatta, went round the country encouraging Africans to take an oath not to help the Whites.

The most powerful tribe in Kenya was the Kikuyu and Kenyatta was one of its leaders. The Kikuyu became impatient when the oath promising not to help Whites did not seem to be enough to force any change. Some of the Kikuyu took another oath to begin murdering Whites and their black helpers. This movement was called Mau Mau and in October 1952, after a series of murders, Kenyatta and five other leaders of KAU were arrested as those suspected of leading Mau Mau. The arrest of Kenyatta did not stop the

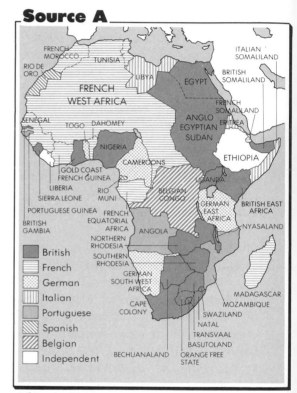

Source A

Africa in 1900.

Source B

The Pan African Congress meeting in Manchester, November 1945.

Source C

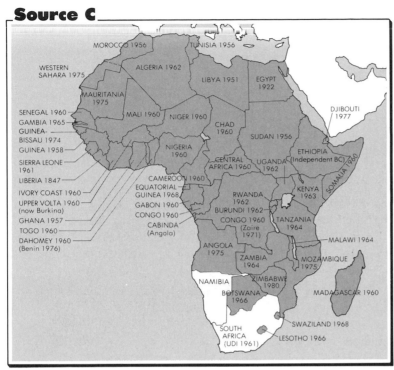

African independence.

Mau Mau. Their attacks increased and they became more organised.

When the Mau Mau were beaten the British hoped to form a multi-racial government, but although some black Africans were made members of the new Legislative Council, by 1959 co-operation had broken down and the Africans walked out. A conference was called in London in 1960 to discuss the future of Kenya. It was decided that Africans should immediately form the majority in the Legislative Assembly, with independence to follow in a few years. The British felt it was better to agree with the Kenyan leaders, Tom Mboya and Ronald Ngala, rather than risk renewed Mau Mau activity.

The Kenyans prepared for independence (Uhuru) and Kenyatta was released from prison in 1961. He became leader of the KANU political party in 1962 (Kenya African National Union). When Kenya was finally given independence in December 1963 Kenyatta became the first Prime Minister.

Source D

'The Mau Mau gangs lived in the forests. They copied army uniforms and called their leaders "generals". They made guns out of metal pipes. At night they crept into the fields for food. Police ports were raided and arms taken....'

From 'Kenyatta', by P. Ripley, 1972.

Source E

'God said this is our land in which we are to flourish as a nation. We are not worried that other races are here with us in our country, but we say we are the leaders here, and what we want we insist we get. We want our cattle to grow fat on our land so that our children grow up in prosperity; we do not want that fat to feed others.'

Jomo Kenyatta, from a speech at a KAU rally, 1951.

Questions

Section A

1 a Study Source C. Which was the first black African country to achieve independence? Which was the last?

 b Draw a time-line to show the movement to independence in Africa.

 c Do you think there was a key **turning-point** in the events shown on your time-line? If so, when? Give reasons for your answer.

2 a What was the date of the Pan African Congress?

 b What were its aims as revealed in Source B?

3 What were the reasons suggested by British and other colonial powers to postpone independence for African countries?

Section B

4 Study Sources D and E. Why did Kenyatta and the Mau Mau believe power-sharing with the Whites was wrong?

5 In one area of Africa, South Africa, power is held by Whites only. How do you think the events in this unit would be viewed by:

 a white South Africans?

 b black South Africans?

54

Africa (ii): South Africa and Apartheid

From the middle of the eighteenth century the Dutch began to settle in southern Africa around the Cape of Good Hope. In 1795 the Cape was seized by the British and, in 1833, when Britain passed anti-slavery laws throughout the empire, the Dutch – known as Boers – decided to move away from the Cape to free themselves from British control. The 'Great Trek' was a time of hardship for the Boers. Many were killed in attacks by Africans. War broke out between the British and the Boers in 1899 and, although the Boers were beaten by 1902, they still outnumbered the British. Britain joined the two Boer Republics to its own provinces. This meant that when South Africa became a self-governing dominion within the British Empire it was dominated by the Boers or **Afrikaners** (white Africans) as they now called themselves.

South Africa is a country rich in natural resources. Gold was discovered in the Transvaal, and Johannesburg attracted thousands of white settlers. They did not like working alongside Africans and the dirty and dangerous jobs in goldmines were given to black workers who were made to live in compounds. These workers often came from the countryside or neighbouring countries like Mozambique and were forced to leave their families at home.

This idea of remaining separate from black Africans was soon government policy. After the Second World War, in 1948, the National Party came to power and developed a policy of racial separation known as **Apartheid**. The policy claimed to aim at separate development for Blacks and Whites but, in practice, it was based on the belief that Whites were, and would always be, superior to Blacks. All the best jobs and government positions were reserved for Whites and the system of Apartheid kept white and black living areas apart.

Blacks (the Bantu) were forced on to 'homelands'. There were nine of these but they covered only 13 per cent of South Africa's land and were in the worst areas for agriculture. The first 'Bantustan' (homeland) was created in 1963, but it was miles from the cities where most black people worked. As a result the South African government built black townships outside the cities and forced workers to travel into work each day on trains.

To be able to travel into the cities black people needed passes. The pass laws began in 1952 and controlled black Africans' lives. The pass stated how long a black person

An example of Apartheid.

Scene at Sharpeville, 1960.

'It's over boys. This country will never be the same again. They'll want revenge for this. Now the black man has been given a cause.'

News reporter on the 'Rand Daily Mail'.

Source C

'Our fight is against poverty and lack of human dignity. Africans want to be paid a living wage. We want to live where we can obtain work, and not be sent away because we weren't born there. Our women want to be with their menfolk and not left in the reserves [Bantustans]. We want to be allowed out after 11 o'clock at night, and not be confined to our rooms like little children.... I have fought against white domination, and I have fought against black domination. I want a society in which all persons live together in harmony. For this I am prepared to die.'

Nelson Mandela, July 1963.

Source D

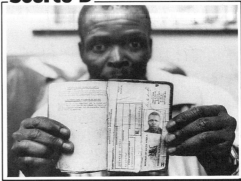

An African shows his pass.

could stay in a city and had to be carried at all times in case police officers asked to see it.

A black political party, the African National Congress (ANC), campaigned against Apartheid and for equal rights. As early as 1956 its leaders were imprisoned, and a campaign against pass laws in the 1960s failed. Non-violent opposition to Apartheid did not affect the government. In 1960, in the black township of Sharpeville, police opened fire on a non-violent demonstration and killed sixty-seven Africans.

In 1963, the Ninety-Day Law was passed, which allowed police to arrest suspected black 'trouble makers' and keep them in detention. At the end of ninety days the suspects were to be released but could immediately be re-arrested. One of the main reasons for the law was the work of an organisation called 'The Spear of the Nation' led by a black African, Nelson Mandela. 'Spear' had petrol-bombed white businesses and attacked Whites at home as a demonstration against Apartheid. On 11 July 1963, Mandela was arrested and, with six others, sentenced to life imprisonment. At his trial Mandela explained the grievances of Blacks (Source C).

Opposition to Apartheid has continued both in and out of South Africa. In 1963 the United Nations imposed an embargo on arms sales to South Africa. Because of segregation in sport South Africa was banned from the Olympic movement in 1968 and has few sporting links with foreign countries. The ANC began to train in guerrilla tactics in neighbouring states and launched violent attacks on South Africa in the 1970s. In 1976, in Soweto, police again opened fire on a non-violent demonstration when school students protested against being taught lessons in the Afrikaans language. More than 500 Blacks were killed in the disturbances which followed. In the 1980s the violence has increased. In 1985 more police shootings led to ANC bomb attacks in Johannesburg shopping centres and the house arrest of Winnie Mandela, wife of Nelson Mandela. In 1986, other countries imposed economic sanctions on South Africa and leading international companies withdrew, but as yet there is no end to the Apartheid system.

Questions

Section A

1 Briefly describe and explain the following:

   a The Great Trek.
   b The Boer War.
   c Bantustans.
   d The African National Congress.

2 What is Apartheid? How does it work?

3 a Draw a time-line to show the events in this unit.
   b Compare your time-line with the one showing the events in the rest of Africa over the same period (from Unit 53). What are the main differences? Why do you think events have developed differently in South Africa?

Section B

4 Do you think the extract from the *Rand Daily Mail* was written by a white reporter for a white newspaper, or a black reporter for a black newspaper? Give reasons for your answer.

5 'Foreigners in our own country'. Study Sources A and D. Why would black Africans feel this way in South Africa?

6 Black and white South Africans both think of South Africa as their home. Does this similarity in their ideas mean they are likely to solve their problems and live together in peace? Explain your answer.

55

India Since Independence

In 1946, riots throughout India convinced the British government it should hand over all power to an independent India. By August 1947 British rule had ended. The end of British rule sparked off fighting between Hindus, Muslims and Sikhs and the only solution seemed to be to partition (divide) the country and to create the separate Muslim state of West and East Pakistan. The Muslim leader, Mohammed Ali Jinnah, said there was no way to force unity where none was wanted. There was further fighting between the new India and Pakistan over Kashmir in 1949, with the result that that state was also divided between the two countries.

On 30 January 1948, Mahatma Gandhi, who had worked tirelessly for an independent India, was assassinated by Hindu extremists. They believed Gandhi had betrayed India by agreeing to the creation of Pakistan. After Gandhi's death, his successor as leader of the Congress Party was his long-time friend and colleague, Jawaharlal Nehru. Nehru was determined to lead India as a modern democratic state, and, until his death in 1964, considerable progress was made. Living standards rose, the power of princes and of the caste system was reduced, and women were given full civil rights. By the early 1960s, however, India's rapidly growing population had caused an end to the rise in living standards. The population rose from 360,000,000 at the time of independence to over 500,000,000 by 1968. The problems connected with slowing down this rate of growth were enormous. India had a tradition of large families which were seen as the basis of wealth, about 80 per cent of the population was illiterate, and there were more than sixty languages spoken in the country. Large-scale attempts at family planning were backed by the government and had some success, but the population had grown to well over 600,000,000 by 1980.

In 1966 Mrs Indira Gandhi (Nehru's daughter) was elected as Prime Minister. Under her leadership, India became one of the most technologically advanced countries of the Third World. Six space satellites, all made in India, were launched to improve weather forecasting and telecommunications. Indian scientists suceeded in splitting the atom, and India built its own missiles and planes. Despite her achievements, however, Mrs Gandhi struggled in vain to improve the living standards of the majority of Indians. The caste system continued to act as a barrier to equal opportunities, and Mrs Gandhi herself was accused of corrupt election practices

Source A

'Gandhiji has been killed by his own people for whose redemption he lived. This is a second crucifixion in the history of the world.... Father, forgive us.'

From the 'Hindustan Standard', 31 January 1948.

Source B

Non-aligned conference in Delhi

The conference was opened by the Cuban head of state Fidel Castro in 1979. After the opening address the Indian Prime Minister, Mrs Indira Gandhi, took the chair. She did not oppose the final communiqué which sharply attacked the West and in particular the United States. Mrs Gandhi emphasised the deteriorating position of the Third World with over 30 million unemployed, foreign debts which had doubled since 1979 to 600 billion dollars, balance of payments deficits totalling 100 billion dollars, exports falling by 40 billion dollars in the past two years and prices of raw materials at their lowest for 50 years. Faced with this situation Mrs Gandhi called upon the industrialised nations to create a new worldwide economic order.

From the 'International Year Book' 1985.

Source C

during the elections of 1971. For two years, from 1975 to 1977, she declared a state of emergency and imprisoned her critics. Although she gained popularity by a crash programme of irrigation schemes and land redistribution, she was voted out of office after restoring democracy in 1977. But in 1980 she regained power after winning the election.

In the 1980s Mrs Gandhi gained considerable prestige as one of the leaders of the 'non-aligned movement'. This movement is made up of countries, mainly from the Third World, which meet from time to time to assert their independence from the super-powers. Nehru had organised the first meeting of twenty-nine countries in 1955 and by March 1984 ninety-four countries met at Delhi.

Mrs Gandhi did not live to see whether her vision of a new worldwide economic order would be realised. On 31 October 1984 she was assassinated by two Sikh members of her own bodyguard. This was because in June she had agreed to the storming by Indian troops of the sacred Sikh Golden Temple in Amritsar. The Sikhs had continually protested about their treatment by the Hindu majority and a group led by Sant Jamail Singh Bhindranwale had committed several acts of murder and terrorism. They had then taken refuge in the Golden Temple until attacked by the Indian army.

Mrs Gandhi was followed as leader by her son Rajiv and his position was endorsed by his victory in the general election of December 1984. His first task as Prime Minister was to calm the situation in India following his mother's death. In the days immediately after the assassination more than 1500 Sikhs were murdered in retaliation and corpses were found on almost every train travelling into Delhi.

◄ *Mrs Gandhi's body was traditionally burned on a funeral pyre on the banks of the Jamuna River in Delhi. Days later, her son Rajiv, scattered her ashes over the Himalayas from an aeroplane.*

Source D

There are about 12 million Sikhs in India. The Sikh religion was founded in the fifteenth century when one branch of the Hindu religion, unhappy with the caste system, turned to Islam.

The State of Punjab was established in 1966 to satisfy the Sikh majority who lived in the area. But the Sikhs still felt threatened by the Hindu majority elsewhere in India and often there were clashes between them. Bhindranwale's demands included the redistribution of water resources to help the Punjab and a ban on entry to the Golden Temple of Amritsar by non-Sikhs. Bhindranwale's supporters were heavily armed.

Questions

Section A

1 Describe how Hindu–Muslim antagonisms led to the creation of Pakistan and the death of Mahatma Gandhi soon after Indian independence.

2 What problems have been faced by successive Indian governments? Describe how they have been tackled by:
   a Jawaharlal Nehru.
   b Indira Gandhi.

3 What is the non-aligned movement? Why do you think India has been a prominent member of the movement?

Section B

4 Study Source A. What is the attitude of the writer to Mahatma Gandhi? If other Indians shared this attitude, how do you explain Gandhi's assassination in 1948?

5 Study Source B. Mrs Gandhi was an anti-communist. How do you explain her willingness to host the non-aligned movement which includes Marxist states like Cuba?

6 How does Source D help to explain:

   a the importance of religion in Indian politics?
   b the decision by the Indian government to risk the storming of the Golden Temple?

56

The European Economic Community

After the Second World War many western European politicians became convinced that the best way to avoid a future European war was through closer co-operation between countries, not only in military alliances like NATO but also in economic affairs. The Marshall Plan (see page 68) pointed the way as early as 1947, and in 1949 the Council of Europe was formed as a meeting place where problems could be discussed. As confidence grew, progress was made on the economic front and in 1952 France, West Germany, Italy, Belgium, Luxemburg and the Netherlands decided to form the European Coal and Steel Community (ECSC). The union was so successful that in 1957 the six members of the ECSC signed the Treaty of Rome and created the European Economic Community (EEC) which became known as the Common Market.

At first Britain and other European countries did not join the Community, and entered into a looser economic union, the European Free Trade Association (EFTA), which included Austria, Denmark, Norway, Portugal, Sweden and Switzerland. It soon became clear, however, that the EEC was very successful in raising the living standards of people in its member countries, and in 1963 Britain tried to join. Mainly because of opposition from the French President, de Gaulle, the British application was rejected in 1963, and again in 1967.

In 1970, de Gaulle died and French opposition to Britain's entry to the EEC died with him. In January 1972, Britain, Denmark, Eire and Norway signed treaties which allowed them to join the EEC from 1973, but after all four countries had held referenda to test public reaction to joining, Norway withdrew. 'The six' became 'the nine'. In Britain, many people were also against entry because they believed the EEC would limit the sovereignty of the Parliament at Westminster or would damage trade with the Commonwealth. Many also doubted that the prosperity of the EEC could continue after it was enlarged.

During the late 1970s and early 1980s Britain's trade with Europe increased enormously, justifying the claim that Britain's future lay in Europe. However, the doubters continued to point to the failures of the EEC. The Community's regional development fund, set aside to help poorer areas of the Community, was unable to bridge the

Main principles of the Treaty of Rome, 1957

1. The creation of a free trade area for goods, money and workers.
2. Common policies for transport and agriculture.
3. The creation of a 'Common Market' Commission in Brussels to administer the agreement.
4. The creation of a European Parliament, with limited powers.
5. The creation of a European Court of Justice to settle disputes.

'... in the end there would appear a colossal Atlantic community under American dependence and leadership which would soon swallow up the European Community.'

President de Gaulle, 1963.

'I suspect you of driving under the influence of America.'

From 'Punch', 1967.

gap between the poorer and richer areas. The Common Agricultural Policy (CAP) paid out vast sums in subsidies to farmers, particularly in France, and as a result there was huge overproduction leading to 'mountains' of butter, beef, sugar and wheat, together with 'lakes' of wine. In the 1980s, Mrs Thatcher twice threatened to withhold Britain's contributions to the EEC budget unless they could be scaled down from what the British described as 'unfair proportions'.

In the 1980s the Economic Community has not been able to avoid the problem of world recession. 'The nine' have become 'the twelve' with the admission of Spain, Portugal and Greece. Although the average income of western Europeans is among the highest in the world, countries in the EEC still have their economic difficulties. In particular, the problems of enough investment in new industry and of massive unemployment still need to be solved.

Source D

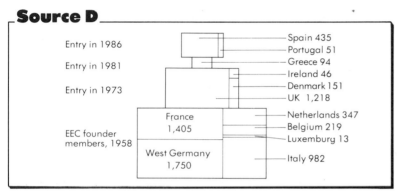

Entry in 1986	Spain 435
	Portugal 51
Entry in 1981	Greece 94
	Ireland 46
Entry in 1973	Denmark 151
	UK 1,218
	France 1,405
	Netherlands 347
EEC founder members, 1958	Belgium 219
	Luxemburg 13
	West Germany 1,750
	Italy 982

Growth and investment 1972–82.

Source E

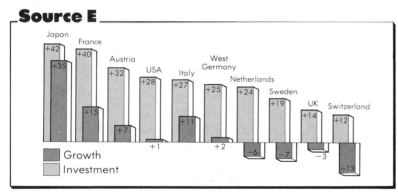

	Japan	France	Austria	USA	Italy	West Germany	Netherlands	Sweden	UK	Switzerland
Growth	+35	+15	+7	+1	+11		+2	−6	−3	−13
Investment	+42	+40	+32	+28	+27	+25	+24	+19	+14	+12

Growth of the EEC in 1000 million DM.

Source F

	1978	1979	1980	1981	1982
Belgium	8.4	8.7	9.3	11.6	13.9
Great Britain	5.7	5.3	6.9	10.2	12.2
France	5.2	6.0	6.5	7.8	8.3
Italy	7.1	7.5	8.0	8.6	9.9
Netherlands	4.1	4.1	4.9	7.3	10.4
West Germany	3.9	3.4	3.4	4.8	6.9
Average in EEC	5.5	5.5	6.1	7.8	9.4

Percentage of unemployment in western Europe, 1978–82.

Questions

Section A

1 What do the following terms and initials mean?

   a ECSC, b EFTA, c EEC, d referendum, e sovereignty, f CAP

2 Why did Britain not join the EEC until 1973?

3 a In what ways has the EEC been a success?
   b In what ways has the EEC been a failure?

Section B

4 Compare Sources B and C.

   a What reason do they both suggest lay behind President de Gaulle's opposition to British entry to the EEC?
   b How might a historian be able to check whether the sources are correct?

5 Study Source D.

   a Which countries were the last to be admitted to the EEC?
   b In which year was Greece admitted as a member?
   c How does the source suggest that the original six members are the most prosperous?

6 a Which EEC members are included in Source E?
   b The EEC has been described both as a 'rich man's club' and a 'fool's paradise'. How does Source E support both judgements?

7 Study Source F.

   a Which EEC country has been most successful in the fight to control unemployment?
   b Does a comparison of Source E with Source F suggest an explanation of the relatively poorer performances of Britain and the Netherlands in controlling unemployment?

8 Sources D, E and F are statistics. Are statistics more useful to historians than other types of source? Explain your answer.

113

57

Northern Ireland (i): Why Did Trouble Break Out In 1968?

The histories of England and Ireland have been linked since at least the twelfth century, when Henry II became the first English king to claim also to be Lord of Ireland. After the Reformation (in the sixteenth century) most English people were Protestants, but most Irish remained Roman Catholics. At the time this often caused political problems. To try to make sure Ireland stayed loyal, the English 'planted' colonies of Protestants in Ireland, especially in Ulster. During the eighteenth and nineteenth centuries Ireland was a poor country and most people were poor workers living on the land. They were also Catholics. Their rich landlords were often Protestants. Irish attempts to win independence from England were crushed until the early twentieth century, often with the leaders of the attempts being seen as heroic martyrs by the Catholic Irish. Not all of Ireland wanted independence though. Protestants were afraid they would suffer in a Catholic country, and felt they had to strengthen ties with England. After Ireland hovered on the edge of civil war for some time a Partition was agreed. Most of Ireland, the 'South', became an independent country called Eire; one part, the 'North', which was most of the old province of Ulster, stayed as part of the United Kingdom.

Northern Ireland had its own parliament and politics were dominated by one party, the Unionists (so called because they were in favour of union with Britain). There were many Roman Catholics living in Northern Ireland. While the population of the province as a whole was 65 per cent Protestant, in some counties, such as county Fermanagh, Roman Catholics outnumbered Protestants. The Unionist party was closely linked to the **Orange Order**, which was a society of Protestants dedicated to keeping Northern Ireland Protestant and British. The combination of Unionism and the Orange Order stopped Catholics from having a fair deal in Northern Ireland, and in the years leading up to 1968 resentment grew in the Catholic community about the way they were being treated.

Catholics felt they had little chance in Northern Ireland. The parliament and the local councils were firmly in the hands of the Unionists. Protestants got more and better council houses and jobs. Even the police were Protestant and not sympathetic towards Catholics. In the late 1960s groups who wanted peaceful reform grew up inside the Catholic community.

Source A

In County Fermanagh no senior posts (and relatively few other) were held by Catholics; this was explained by reference to proven loyalty [to the Union] as a necessary test for Local Authority appointments. In that county, among seventy-five drivers of school buses, at most seven were Catholics.

Council housing policy has also been distorted for political ends in the Unionist controlled areas. In each houses have been built and allocated in such a way that they will not disturb the political balance.

The basic complaint is that in some areas the electoral system is weighted against the non-Unionists, and the complaint is justified.... In County Fermanagh a Catholic majority in the population was converted into a large Unionist majority on the Council.

Extracts from the report of an official investigation into the state of Northern Ireland, the Cameron Commission, 1969.

Source B

Living conditions in the Catholic Bogside area of Londonderry: Mr Patrick Doherty and his daughter in the backyard of their home.

Source C

A march in support of reform is broken up by fighting at Burntollet Bridge.

Source D

'And then we came to Burntollet Bridge, and from the lanes at each side of the road a curtain of bricks and boulders and bottles brought the march to a halt. From the lanes burst hordes of screaming people wielding planks of wood, bottles, laths, iron bars, crowbars, cudgels studded with nails, and they waded into the march beating hell out of everybody. The attackers were beating marchers into the ditches, and across the ditches into the river. I saw a young fellow getting a thrashing from four or five Paisleyites [followers of the Protestant politician Ian Paisley], with a policeman looking on. A few policemen were at least trying to stop us from being killed, but the others were quite delighted that we were getting what they thought we deserved. I went rampaging up the road saying that if I had my way, not one solitary policeman who was at Burntollet would live to be sorry for what he had done.'

From Bernadette Devlin, 'The Price of My Soul'. Devlin was one of the leaders of the demonstration which was attacked at Burntollet Bridge.

Questions

Section A

1 Write a short paragraph explaining what you understand by each of these terms:

   a Unionist.
   b Orange Order.
   c Eire.
   d Northern Ireland.

2 One of the main political differences between Irish people is whether or not they think Ireland should be linked with Britain. How did this political difference come to be connected with a religious difference?

3 Why do you think Northern Ireland remained linked to Britain when Eire became an independent country?

4 a Does the Cameron Commission report (Source A) suggest the Catholic community in Northern Ireland was justified in thinking things were not fair in the 1960s?
   b Is there any reason to suspect the Cameron Commission might have been biased?

5 What can you say about living conditions in the Catholic community from Source B?

6 a The fight at Burntollet Bridge was one of a number of clashes between Catholics, Protestants and the police. On the basis of Sources C and D, what do you think happened there?
   b Do you think your description of what happened at Burntollet Bridge is reliable? Give reasons for your answer.

Section B

7 Ireland is often said to be a country that suffers for its history. How far back in Irish history do you think historians need to go to explain the causes of the 'troubles' which began in 1968?

8 Bernadette Devlin claimed she wanted the march at Burntollet Bridge to be peaceful. Does this mean:

   a she was lying?
   b what people want to happen is irrelevant in history?
   c What people want to happen is important, but other things influence what finally happens?

   Pick **one** of these alternatives and explain why you think it is right.

9 How do you think the events of Burntollet Bridge will have affected the attitudes of the marchers to the police?

10 Do you think the events of Burntollet Bridge have any importance to what is happening in Northern Ireland now? Explain your answer.

58

Northern Ireland (ii): The 1970s and 1980s

The Civil Rights protests of 1968 had often ended in violence. The violence increased in the following years. It became clear that the Catholic community did not trust the police, especially the B Specials, part-time police officers drawn almost entirely from the Protestant community. In July 1969 fighting between B Specials and Catholic protesters in Belfast got out of hand. Six people were killed and 150 houses burned in the Catholic area of the city. The British government decided it would have to use the army to keep law and order in Northern Ireland.

In August 1971, with violence increasing, the British government introduced **internment** (imprisonment without trial) when people were suspected of being terrorists. This made matters worse as the terrorist groups reacted with more violence. By this stage the conflict had outgrown the reforming organisations of the 1960s. The **Irish Republican Army (IRA)** and the **Provisional IRA (Provos)** attacked the army and Protestants in the name of uniting Ireland. Protestant terrorist groups, such as the **Ulster Volunteer Force (UVF)** attacked Catholics and the army in the name of preserving the Union with Britain.

Throughout the 1970s and into the 1980s no peace movement has ever been able to gain much support for long. Moves by politicians have also failed to find a way out of the crisis. There are many people in both communities who believe absolutely in their cause. In 1981 Provisional IRA men, in prison for terrorist activities, went on hunger strike. They demanded to be treated as political prisoners not criminals. Ten men starved themselves to death before the protest ended. Events like this help to convince many people that their side is right. To their supporters the hunger strikers were martyrs and the incident showed how unfeeling the British government was. To their opponents it showed what fanatical and dangerous men the hunger strikers were.

In 1985 the British and Eire governments signed the Anglo–Irish Agreement in another attempt to find a political solution. This agreement gives the Eire government a say in the running of Northern Ireland. It has been fiercely opposed by both Unionists and Republicans.

Source A

'The Army moved in and battered its way up the Shankhill with bloodthirsty enthusiasm. In the shooting two Protestants were killed and a dozen wounded. Many others were beaten or kicked unconscious. Who in the Bogside could doubt that at last law and order were being administered impartially?'

A description of a Protestant demonstration in 1970 from Eamon McCann's 'War and an Irish Town'. McCann had been a leader of Catholic Civil Rights protests since 1968.

Source B

'Thirty doors in the Old Park district of Belfast splintered and burst open under the onslaught of Army fury and boots. Over a hundred people turfed out of bed. Screams, yells, thuds, all shatter the morning stillness. The elderly, the infirm, the young, the tired, and the lonely.
"English pigs!"
"Para bastards, youse animals!"
"I've got a heart condition, she's got epilepsy."
"Youse broke my door!"
The abuse is never ending, the quality never changing. Now it just rolls off my back and I concentrate on the job.

A week ago, one of our section commanders was hit in the stomach by a sniper's bullet, just thirty yards from this house. He was lucky, he managed to get to hospital and the operating theatre. The locals cheered at the time.

The dwellings, one could hardly call them houses, were typical of the ghettos of Belfast, with two rooms upstairs, two down, an outside toilet. An assortment of sweating humanity lived in sordid conditions of filth.'

From A.F.N. Clarke, 'Contact' – a soldier's account of his service in Northern Ireland.

Source C

In memory of Patrick

KILLED AUGUST 15, 1969

TIME has not healed the anguish of Neely and Alice Rooney.

It has merely allowed them strength enough to discuss that terrible night in August, 1969, without breaking down.

They are still haunted by the shock and the horror of the night a stray bullet penetrated a bedroom wall, striking their nine-year-old son in the head.

"Sometimes when there's only the two of us here we sit and have a good cry just thinking of him," says Alice.

"Not that we're the only ones round here to have lost a child."

Patrick—the first child to die in the Ulster troubles—was a victim of the now-disbanded auxiliary force, the B-Specials, who opened fire on Belfast's Divis Flats where the Rooneys lived.

Two years later Alice, who had five other children, gave birth to another boy, also called Patrick, who now sits across from his parents listening quietly to stories of the other Patrick, who dreamed of becoming a priest.

But this Patrick is full of street-cunning.

"Over there," he says, pointing to a barricade, "that's where me and me mates throw stones at Prods."

"Why?" you ask him. He looks up for a second and then shrugs . . . as though the question is too soft to answer.

Patrick is not her only loss. Her sister, she tells you, was killed by a bullet meant for someone else. Her nephew was blown to bits by a bomb.

VICTIMS: The Rooneys with the second Patrick.

From a story in the 'Daily Mirror', 15 August 1984.

Source D

A terrorist's funeral in Northern Ireland.

Questions

Section A

1 Write a sentence or two explaining what you understand by the following:

   a Provos.   c UDF.
   b IRA.   d Terrorism.

2 Why did the British government send the army into Northern Ireland?

3 a What was the 1981 Provisional IRA hunger strike?
   b Why do you think events like this are important?

Section B

4 How do you think the Catholic community felt about the arrival of British troops in 1969?

5 How do you think the following would feel about the family in Source C?
   a A supporter of the Provos   b A supporter of the UVF

   c A British soldier on duty in Northern Ireland

6 How do you think the following would feel about the scene shown in Source D?

   a A supporter of the Provos
   b A supporter of the UVF
   c A British soldier on duty in Northern Ireland

7 How important do you think people's attitudes are in the current situation in Northern Ireland?

59

Sources for Twentieth-Century History

Historians working on the twentieth century have different problems from those working on much earlier periods. To take an extreme example, a historian working on Ancient Greece may have studied almost all the sources that survive on a particular topic. This could not be the case for a historian studying a twentieth-century problem like the causes of the Second World War. So much survives in newspapers, letters, diaries, government papers, books written at the time and by later historians that one person could not hope to study them all.

The key word in the last sentence was **survives**. We are still living in the twentieth century and much less of the material will have been destroyed either by chance or on purpose. There was, of course, more of it to start with. Newspapers, for instance, have existed in Britain since the seventeenth century but only in the last hundred years or so have they been cheap enough to be bought and read by most people.

This is not all. The historian of the twentieth century has access to types of source that do not exist for earlier periods. The most obvious source is sometimes called **oral history** – talking to people who were there at the time. Obviously this souce is only available for the lifespan of the possible witnesses, and there are few people left who can remember life in the nineteenth century. You may have looked at some of the strengths and weaknesses of oral evidence in the exercise on page 50. Film, radio, and television are also sources not available to historians of earlier periods.

People in the twentieth century are used to getting their news much faster than ever happened before, and often seeing or hearing things happen as well. In Britain in 1939 people heard the Prime Minister explain the reasons for the declaration of war against Germany on the radio. In weekly newsreels at the cinema they could see the events they had heard about in the last week. Later, television brought these pictures into people's homes every day. Big events that interest people in many countries, like the Olympic Games or a meeting between President Reagan and Mr Gorbachev, are seen by millions of people across the world.

Film, radio and television, however, are really new ways of spreading old sources – news, plays and stories. Very often these sources tell us as much by accident as they tell us on purpose. On the opposite page are some extracts from the *Daily Sketch* for 12 April 1928. The intention was to tell the

Questions

1 As what, according to the headline, was 'Big Bill' Thompson trying to be elected?

2 a Who, according to the story, were the candidates in the election for Mayor of Chicago?
   b Who, according to the story, was **not** a candidate in the election for the Mayor of Chicago?

3 Read pages 28 – 9. Why do you think gangsters were so important in the Chicago election?

4 What do you think the *Daily Sketch* thought about:

   a 'Big Bill' Thompson?
   b the way people lived and acted in the USA?

5 What can you tell about the clothes people wore in 1928 from these extracts?

6 What can you tell about attitudes to women in 1928 from these extracts?

7 Compare these extracts with a modern newspaper. What differences are there?

8 Do you think the *Daily Sketch's* account of the election in Chicago is completely reliable? Give reasons for your answer.

9 Do you think all the news stories in today's papers are completely reliable? Explain your answer using examples.

Extracts from the 'Daily Sketch', 12 April 1928. ▶

Source A

CHICAGO REJECTS ANTI-BRITISH MAYOR

"Big Bill" Thompson Defeated

Wild Scenes in Election Fight: One Man Killed, Two Wounded and Six Kidnapped: Gangs' Pitched Battle With Pistols

All indications are that in a record poll "Big Bill" Thompson, Chicago's anti-British mayor, has been heavily defeated.

One candidate killed, six persons kidnapped and two wounded were the casualties in the most exciting election day Chicago has known.

The presence of 5,000 special police patrolling the city, in addition to the normal police force of Chicago, the whole strength of which was on duty, did not prevent wild scenes in many wards.

Two gangs fought a pitched battle with pistols, and gunmen toured the polling booths attempting to drive away opposition.

Despite the efforts of the gunmen and "gangsters," citizens refused to be wholly intimidated.

news but historians can find out much more than what happened in the Chicago election. The paper gives all sorts of insights into the standard of living, fashion, what people thought was normal and what they thought was acceptable. This use of a source as evidence about things it was not intended for is often very valuable.

All the new sources set historians the same old problems. Are they reliable? Newspapers are often biased and present one side of the story. Film can be edited to give a false impression of what happened. Also, some of the sources may be deliberately hidden. In Britain sensitive government papers are kept from historians for up to one hundred years, and most papers for thirty years. Of the sources that we do have, many may never have had access to the right information. You can ask anybody who was alive at the time why Britain joined the Second World War, but only those people who knew what was said in the Cabinet could give an accurate answer—and they might not choose to.

This Unit looks at some of the advantages, and some of the problems, of the sources historians use when working on the history of the twentieth century.

The assassination of President Kennedy, 1963.

Lee Harvey Oswald was accused of President Kennedy's assassination, but before he could be tried, Oswald was shot and killed by Jack Ruby, a nightclub owner.

Source C

Source D

'I felt the unusual loveliness of our gardens and meadows and hills has come home to us as you see so many women now staring at their soldier husbands, sweethearts, sons, just before the trains take them away. It's as if the English landscape said: "Look at me, as I am now in my beauty and fullness of joy, and do not forget." And when I feel like this, I feel, too, a sudden and very sharp anger; for I remember, then, how this Island is threatened and menaced; how perhaps at this very moment, thin-lipped and cold-eyed Nazi staff officers are planning, with that mixture of method and lunacy which is all their own, how to project onto this countryside of ours those half-doped crazy lads they call parachute troops. This land that is ours, that appeals to us now in all its beauty, is at this moment only just outside the reach of these self-tormenting schemers and their millions who are used as if they were not human beings but automata, robots, mere "things". They drop them from planes as if they were merely bombs with arms and legs. They send them swarming forward in battle as if they were not fellowmen but death-dealing dolls, manufactured in Goering's factories....

The rest of us have simply to stand up and say: "NO!" If we do that firmly, and cheerfully, and throw all our energy into the task of making the "No" decisive, these people are done for. The Nazis understand – and it is their great secret – all the contemptible qualities of men. They have a lightning eye for an opponent's weakness. But what they don't understand, because there is nothing in their nature or experience to tell them, is that men also have their hours of greatness, when weakness suddenly towers into strength; when ordinary easy-going men rise in their anger and strike down evil like the angels of the wrath of God.'

From a wartime radio talk given by J.B. Priestley, Sunday 9 June 1940.

Questions

Section A

1 The photographs on the opposite page allow you to see what actually happened at two infamous moments in the history of the last thirty years. Copy out the following questions and try to answer them for each of the two incidents.

Incident:

- What happened to the victim?

- Who are the people closest to the victim?

- What is the reaction of the people close to the victim?

- Can you see what direction the attack came from?

- Can you see any attackers? If so, describe them and explain why you think they were attackers.

- Can you see what the **motives** of the attackers were?

2 Do you think the photographs are more use in trying to work out what happened to Kennedy or to Oswald?

3 The assassination of President Kennedy came as a great shock to most people. You can use it as a basis for an oral history exercise. Ask three different people alive in 1963:

  a Can you remember what you were doing on 22 November 1963?
  b Can you remember what you were doing when you heard that President Kennedy had been assassinated?
  c How did you feel when you heard President Kennedy had been assassinated?
  d Do you know who assassinated President Kennedy and why?

4 Do you think it would be fair to say that J.B. Priestley was biased against the Germans?

5 What will interest a historian most about the extract from Priestley's talk: whether it is right or wrong about German planning or the fact the radio talk was heard by millions of people in Britain one Sunday evening?

Section B

6 What advantages does a historian get from the photographs, films and radio and television recordings that are available for the study of the twentieth century?

7 What problems will these new sources present to historians?

8 What things do you think oral sources will be useful for?

Details of written sources

In some instances, the full details of the written sources have not been included in the text. These are given below.

Unit 2
Sources B, D and F: From Malcolm Brown, *Tommy Goes to War* (Dent, 1978).
Source E: George Coppard, *With a Machine Gun to Cambrai* (Imperial War Museum/ Jane's Publishing Company, 1980).

Unit 4
Source A: Robert Graves, *Goodbye to All That* (Penguin, 1969).
Source D: George Coppard, *With a Machine Gun to Cambrai* (Imperial War Museum/Jane's, 1980).

Unit 6
Source A: Harry Mills, *Twentieth-Century World History in Focus* (Macmillan, 1984).
Source E: Vera Brittain, *Testament of Youth* (Gollancz, 1933)

Unit 9
Source A: John Reed, *Ten Days That Shook the World* (Penguin, 1970).

Unit 10
Source A: From J. E. O'Connor, *The Sokolov Investigation* (Souvenir Press, 1972).

Unit 11
Source A: George Orwell, *The Road to Wigan Pier* (Penguin, 1970).

Unit 12
Source C: From Lionel Kochan, *The Making of Modern Russia* (Jonathan Cape, 1962).
Source D: N. Lowe, *Mastering Modern World History* (Macmillan, 1982).

Unit 13
Source C: George Brown, *In My Way* (Gollancz, 1971).
Source G: From the *Kentish Gazette*, May 1926.

Unit 14
Source A: Senator J. L. Sheppard, quoted in John Kobler, *Ancient Spirits* (Michael Joseph, 1974).

Unit 15
Source D: Eleanor Roosevelt, *Autobiography*.

Unit 16
Sources A, B and C: Quoted in Christopher Leeds, *Italy Under Mussolini* (Wayland, 1972).

Unit 19
Sources B and G: Agnes Smedley, *Chinese Destinies: Sketches of Present Day China* (Hurst & Blackett, 1934).

Unit 23

Source A: Quoted in Philip Toynbee, *The Distant Drum* (Sidgwick & Jackson, 1976).

Sources B and E: Gordon Thomas and Max Morgan-Witts, *The Day Guernica Died* (Hodder & Stoughton, 1975).

Unit 24

Source A: Tom Harrisson and Charles Madge (eds.), *Britain by Mass Observation*, 1939.

Unit 25

Source F: H. R. Trevor-Roper (ed.) *Hitler's War Directives, 1939–45* (Sidgwick & Jackson, 1964).

Unit 26

Sources B and D: H. R. Trevor-Roper (ed.), *Hitler's War Directives, 1939–45* (Sidgwick & Jackson, 1964).

Source C: A. J. P. Taylor, 'The False Alliance' in Purnell's *History of the Twentieth Century*.

Source E: Quoted in *War Speeches, Orders of the Day and Answers to Foreign Press Correspondents during the Great Patriotic War by Generalissimo Stalin* (Hutchinson, 1945).

Unit 28

Source A: Peter Calvocoressi, *Top Secret Ultra* (Cassell, 1980).

Source D: Denis Wheatley, *The Deception Planners: My Secret War* (Hutchinson, 1980).

Unit 29

Source E: From 'Report on Conditions in the Concentration Camps of Oswieccim and Birkenau', Foreign Office Papers, 1944 (HMSO).

Unit 30

Source C: Michihiko Hachiya, *Hiroshima Diary* (Gollancz, 1955).

Unit 41

Source B: Desmond King-Hele, 'Space in the Sixties' in Purnell's *History of the Twentieth Century*.

Unit 42

Source A: Agnes Smedley, 'The Great Road' in *Monthly Review Press*, 1956.

Source B: Dick Wilson, *The Long March* (Hamish Hamilton, 1971).

Unit 43

Sources C and D: Quoted in D. Horowitz (ed.), *Containment and Revolution* (Blond, 1967).

Unit 45

Source B: Tony Howarth, *Twentieth-Century History* (Longman, 1979).

Unit 53

Source D: P. Ripley, *Kenyatta* (Longman, 1972).

Unit 57

Source D: Bernadette Devlin, *The Price of My Soul* (André Deutsch, 1969).

Unit 58

Source A: Eamon McCann, *War and an Irish Town* (Pluto Press, 1980).

Source B: A.F.N. Clarke, *Contact* (Secker & Warburg, 1983).